COSMOSIS

THE TECHNIQUE
AND ITS USE IN
DAILY LIVING

COSMOSIS

THE TECHNIQUE AND ITS USE
IN DAILY LIVING

Kingdon L. Brown

Parker Publishing Company, Inc.
West Nyack, New York

PRINTED IN THE UNITED STATES OF AMERICA
ISBN 0-13-179754-9
B&P

Dedicated to the New Age
and its messengers of
revealed truth.

What This Book Can Do for You

Every life is controlled by the hidden energy of the universe. For centuries mankind has been studying this energy in order to unlock its psychic secrets—the secrets that lead to a life of real happiness.

Today many people are using this higher power for their own benefit. They have unlocked the secrets of the eternal creative force, *Cosmosis!* These people, many of them just like yourself, are happy, prosperous, and healthy because they have let Cosmosis work for them.

Cosmosis-directed people stand out in any crowd. They are the leaders, the people with personal magnetism and abundant "good luck."

With this book, you have at your command the first real guide to the ancient art of Cosmosis. You will learn how this tremendous power can go to work for you with just a few minutes of daily conditioning! You can set this *universal energy* into motion and it will dynamically bring *your desires* into complete and *total* manifestation—without further effort on your part.

Think of it! Nothing can stop your progress to the top. You can banish unproductive circumstances and unprofitable situations *forever.* You can literally become the luckiest person you know.

Fate will become the secret weapon for good in your life.

7

Cosmosis will even show you the easy way to alter your future actions so *you can take advantage of events even before they take place.* That's how secure you will be with this Universal Force working for you.

The riches of this life are waiting for you, too. Power, wealth, and real dominance can only be manifested through the eternal creative power of Cosmosis. With it you will conquer all of that which previously appeared invincible to you. You will *have* what you need. You will *be* what you want to be. And, you will do what *you* want to do!

First, you will feel the uplifting presence of Cosmosis. Then, you will see and experience the fantastic results of its renewing, regenerating, and multiplying work in your life.

Great thinkers throughout history have known of Cosmosis. But, never has it been explained in the easy, step-by-step way that you will find in this book. Here, for the very first time, the secrets of Cosmosis are presented *in a way that you can use.*

This book gives you the keys, techniques, and easy methods which others have employed to absorb psychic powers for happy and dynamic living. You will witness how others have *mastered all circumstances* with Cosmosis. You will advance to the point where you can also focus and direct psychic powers instantly.

This book will show *you* how to be a dynamic person. It is all done with the transforming energy of the universe, *Cosmosis.*

KINGDON L. BROWN

- hidden energy of the Universe
- eternal creative force, Cosmosis
- ancient art of Cosmosis
- Universal Energy
- Universal Force
- eternal creative power of Cosmosis
- uplifting presence of Cosmosis
- psychic powers
- transforming energy of the universe, Cosmosis.

- tremendous power of the universe
- Universal Power
- Energy Force Field of the Universe
- eternal life energy, Prana
- the energy of the universe

8

Table of Contents

The energy force-field of the universe. Cosmosis and psychic powers. The magic Cosmosis formula you can use instantly. What happens when you attract and focus Cosmosis. Activating Cosmosis for greater psychic power. How Cosmosis helps control your outward experience. The levels of mind through which Cosmosis operates. How a working technique of meditation clears all levels of mind for Cosmosis. Points to remember from this chapter.

How Cosmosis breaks the time-space axis. Know the true meaning of your past. The technique for attunement with the Akashic records. How to read your future clairvoyantly. Seeing major news events before they happen. Creating future events by Cosmosis visualization. How to decide on the proper link or psychic opening. The ritual for creating future

person. How your Cosmosis-directed personality will affect strangers. How to turn your worst enemies into enthusiastic friends. How to encourage people to accept your friendship. Points to remember from this chapter.

What makes people age? How can aging be slowed and reversed? The nutritional keys to the vigor of youth. A quick look at vitamin essentials. What will make anyone old ahead of schedule? The subconscious fountain of youth. Youth and sexual potency. What food halts aging? How to avoid destructive meals. Some common ailments associated with aging which can be overcome. Points to remember from this chapter.

The universal love principle. Finding your true mate the easy way. How to keep a marriage happy with Cosmosis. How the Kundalini exercise can improve your marriage. What to do if you have chosen the wrong mate. Cosmosis steps on how to end an impossible marriage. Cosmosis advice for those who are always single. Points to remember from this chapter.

How to read and understand your seven-year life cycles. How to work with your life cycle. How to plan a goal orientation program that

Chapter 1

HOW TO ACTIVATE COSMOSIS FOR YOUR NEW LIFE

"**I**n the name of God, stop it," she screamed into the telephone. With that Margaret slammed down the receiver, took a tranquilizer, and dialed my number.

The story was fantastic. Margaret's health had failed and she lost her job. She was alone, desperate, and without financial security. She was being hounded by creditors. They wanted their money and she just did not have any.

"What can I do to change my luck?" she asked me.

A dynamic technique for activating Cosmosis was born to meet Margaret's request. She needed psychic powers to create a new, happy life.

Margaret learned how to tap into the tremendous power of the universe and let it work for *her*.

Cosmosis can activate a new life *for you* in the same wonderful way that it transformed Margaret's life, very much for the better.

"Margaret, do you know what happens at birth?" I asked her.

15

"I know that my life started with my first breath, when the delivering doctor spanked me. It's the same for all humans."

"You've just discovered the secret of *Cosmosis*."

She sounded a little bewildered and I didn't blame her, but she *had* stumbled on the source of Universal Power.

THE ENERGY FORCE FIELD OF THE UNIVERSE

"You see, Margaret, the source of all life and energy is the Cosmic, or solar, rays. These rays enter our atmosphere as ionized or condensed particles. These energy particles are both positive and negative. When we breathe, these particles enter our lungs and are used, with oxygen, to burn the energy which keeps our bodies and life going. When you were born, you started your Cosmic journey because you took your first breath of these life-giving particles. We call this eternal life energy, which is in all things, *Prana*. I tried to simplify my explanation because I wanted to teach Margaret how to absorb more Prana and then focus it for the realization of her desire to be happy.

COSMOSIS AND PSYCHIC POWERS

"Cosmosis is the art of awakening the superconscious mind with solar energies. It is derived from Raja Yoga, the ancient art of making alignment with the Supreme Consciousness or Ultimate Reality. Once alignment is made, psychic powers guide the student into a life of personal control over all conditions."

I tried not to make it sound too fantastic. Yet, I *knew of case after case* where a tremendous streak of "good luck" was *directly* caused by Cosmosis. I hoped it would work for Margaret.

16

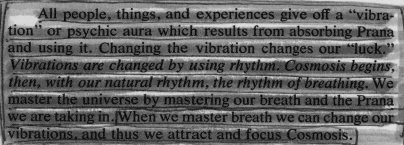

All people, things, and experiences give off a "vibration" or psychic aura which results from absorbing Prana and using it. Changing the vibration changes our "luck." *Vibrations are changed by using rhythm. Cosmosis begins, then, with our natural rhythm, the rhythm of breathing.* We master the universe by mastering our breath and the Prana we are taking in. When we master breath we can change our vibrations, and thus we attract and focus Cosmosis.

Here is a simple breathing exercise which we taught Margaret.

THE MAGIC COSMOSIS FORMULA
YOU CAN USE INSTANTLY

Begin by deciding on the *change* you want in your life. Do you want to eliminate a negative condition? Would you like to attract something beautiful or manifest a secret desire? Be sure you know specifically what adjustments you would like to make. Set aside about 15 minutes for this exercise:

1. *Regular Breathing.* Sit erect, but comfortably, in a chair. Close your eyes slowly and easily. Allow no distractions. Breathe at your regular rate. Bring the air into your lungs. *Hold it for a few seconds.* Discharge it automatically.

2. *Holding the Breath and Focusing the Energy.* As you hold your breath, feel the ionized particles fill your lungs. Feel the energy flowing through your heart and in your bloodstream. Then, see "in your mind's eye" the focusing, or collecting, of this power at the base of your spine.

As the life force is presented to the base of the spine, you will notice that it will begin to ascend or move upward along the spine. This is called the ascent of the *Kundalini.* You may feel hot. You may hear psychic sounds, rhythmic sounds. Or you may see everything around you as a

17

single color. You may feel light-headed or trancelike. Do not be alarmed. You are awakening the psychic centers, the physical counterparts of the higher mental and psychic powers which you are using—perhaps for the first time.

3. *Riding the Mental Crest of the Cosmic Power*. Once you have focused the energy and feel the above sensations, *you are ready to ride the crest of Cosmosis with your desire—the change you need in your life.* (Do not over-stimulate yourself with this exercise. Use it for short periods at first and increase your time as you go along.)

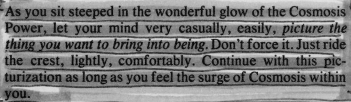

Relax. Do not force your breathing.

Let your breathing return to normal *without the holding period.*

As you sit steeped in the wonderful glow of the Cosmosis Power, let your mind very casually, easily, *picture the thing you want to bring into being.* Don't force it. Just ride the crest, lightly, comfortably. Continue with this picturization as long as you feel the surge of Cosmosis within you.

Continued practice will raise the Kundalini to your head. The strength of the Cosmosis Power will be greater and greater. Do not be disturbed if you sense a gentle, uplifting energy at first. You are better off when you start slowly and build carefully.

How Margaret Changed Her Life with This Magic Formula

Margaret used this simple breathing exercise daily for about three weeks. She visualized a good job, better health, and personal harmony. Within six weeks she had all three.

Today she is one of the best psychic students in our city with a tremendous gift of clairvoyance and a healing power. She is vital, warm, and quite attractive. The change was dramatic and permanent.

WHAT HAPPENS WHEN YOU ATTRACT
AND FOCUS COSMOSIS

This simple Cosmosis formula can be used to gain lasting control over every aspect of your life. With this exercise, you can create the following wonderful conditions for yourself:

1. *Greater Happiness and Harmony*. Mr. S. M. used this simple technique to overcome excessive depression and anxiety. After several weeks, he felt the indwelling "presence" of Cosmosis and he let himself be guided by it.

2. *Self-Healing, Youthful Vigor, and Vitality*. Miss Wilson, a junior high school history teacher, was able to become a star tennis player after using this technique for only a few minutes each day before she went out onto the tennis court to play a game.

3. *Increased Personal Wealth*. Sam, a real estate broker, was able to increase his net value to several hundred thousand dollars by using this technique each day for over a year. He pictured doing the right things, saying the right things, and being at the right places to make the profitable gains he wanted and needed in life.

4. *Greater Love and Appreciation of Life's Blessings*. Nothing can match the reward of knowing that all is working for the outcome of total *good* in your life. Mrs. Smith used this technique to regain true affection from her husband who had been indifferent to her for several years. Today they are a happy, loving couple. They enjoy each minute of every day and they can see the results of Cosmosis in their marriage. They vacation together, plan for their future, and see every opportunity that is presented to them as a step toward greater growth and development.

5. *Better Control of People and Circumstances*. Have you ever had the feeling that nothing was going right? Things were really getting you down, affecting your outlook and

19

never giving you an even break. John R. was a man in his early twenties who had that feeling while he was going through dental school. After practice with the Kundalini he found that he knew where he was going, what he was destined to do, and people just did not bother him so much. He could sail through each day with an optimistic smile and a friendly manner. He was able to manifest his dream, which was to be a successful oral surgeon. He took a beautiful wife, too, and today they live in a beautiful home with their twin boys and a girl.

ACTIVATING COSMOSIS
FOR GREATER PSYCHIC POWER

Psyche is the Greek word for soul. *Psychic insight is the spiritual ability to see or know about the hidden forces of fate,* to direct them and to work with them. Cosmosis is the energy wavelength on which psychic power operates. Clairvoyance, clairaudience, healing, telepathy, mediumship, astral projection, and other extrasensory *demonstrations are caused by the transferring, or changing, of Cosmosis from one vibration or form to another.*

All matter is in vibration and so are all thoughts.

Everything that ever happens is eternally recorded on the Akashic Book of Life.

Jesus was able to change water into wine by rearranging the vibrations through His understanding of the ongoing Cosmosis. The ancient Egyptian alchemists created metals, fluxes, and alloys in the same way—by transmuting the basic structure of metals. The mysteries of chemistry, of atomic power itself, are simply the universal knowledge of Cosmosis as it applies to matter.

Once you dwell in the presence of Cosmosis, you will be able to direct and focus its power for the realization of your hopes, dreams, or desires.

A mental link through concentration must be established with the thing to be influenced. And, once you have successfully activated Cosmosis and let it direct you, to some extent, you will find that the psychic abilities of clairvoyance, healing, telepathy, mediumship, astral projection, and wisdom, once beyond your conscious awareness, will be born within you.

A specific desire may be your starting point. But, your destination in psychic development is the Infinite. You may be surprised, amazed, or delighted with the continuous unfolding of your abilities.

HOW COSMOSIS HELPS CONTROL YOUR OUTWARD EXPERIENCE

Your internal self contains a blueprint of *your* future. You contain a portion of Cosmosis understanding which *creates the experiences you will have in the future*.

Internal understanding, self-knowledge, occurs when you know two things about yourself. Two master keys, as old as creation, can tell you what your *internal self is doing, what it can do, and what it will do for you as your life progresses*.

These two master keys are summed up by the *Law of Karma* which states: Everything you do, say, or think affects that which will happen to you as your life progresses. And everything you do in this existence will affect your future lives.

What are the master keys? These two questions, honestly answered, will help you direct and focus the Cosmosis Power to absorb the psychic energy you need to lead an adjusted, balanced, fulfilling life.

Here are the questions:

First, what is there about yourself that can be changed?

Second, what is there about yourself that cannot be changed?

Cosmosis will help you make the changes that will

make life flow smoothly, effortlessly, and meaningfully. It will also help you live easily with the things that *cannot* be changed.

Cosmosis operates in your life through the various levels of your internal mind. From there the electrical energy charges of your own thought-forms influence the people and circumstances around you.

THE LEVELS OF MIND THROUGH WHICH COSMOSIS OPERATES

Here is how Cosmosis operates to help you absorb psychic power:

1. At the highest level of awareness, Cosmosis influences the *Cosmic Mind* or Divine Mind within you. This is the spark of Eternity or Divinity called the soul. It is part of God or a portion of Infinite Intelligence. It is the causative force in all life.

2. Cosmosis then energizes your *Superconscious Mind.* This is the seat of your extrasensory sending and receiving station. This is the "place" where your subconscious mind is connected with all events, past and future. This is the portion of your being which moves about without respect to your present position in time or space.

3. *Subconscious Mind* is your memory, the originator of dreams, phantasy, and creative imagination. Cosmosis blends into your thought at this point. *But, Cosmosis can energize your subconscious mind either positively or negatively, depending on the inclination of your conscious thought.* That is why it is necessary to do your Cosmosis practice exercises only when you are in an upbeat, positive frame of mind.

4. Your *Conscious Mind* is the receiving point of your reasoning process. Here your five physical senses report what is happening in the physical world. Here you take in

22

data, language, and ordinary perceptions. And, it is here that you reach conclusions. This is the last mental "place" that Cosmosis influences.

The information in this book will help you prepare yourself for the transforming energy of Cosmosis, even in conscious thought—in your actions, decisions, and conclusions.

HOW A WORKING TECHNIQUE OF MEDITATION CLEARS ALL LEVELS OF MIND FOR COSMOSIS

The Cosmosis formula or breathing exercise brings the Universal Force of Cosmosis into your physical body. Next, you'll want to let it supercharge your entire mind as it rises along the spine to your head.

Every thought that enters your mind and every emotional response can be governed by Cosmosis. Here is how it is done:

1. *Feel the Kundalini moving up your spine* slowly as you focus the energy during the breathing exercise.
2. *As the Kundalini ascends the spine, relax, keep your mind passive,* receptive to new inner sounds, feelings, sensations. You may even get visual sensations or impressions.
3. *Return to normal breathing but stay relaxed,* quiet, undisturbed by any outside vibration. Let your thoughts coast, wander. Be alert to promptings from the higher self within. Don't expect anything to happen. But be ready when you begin to feel the Cosmosis energy reach your head, revitalizing all thoughts.
4. *Continue this quiet time* to bring all thoughts and emotions under the direction of peaceful Cosmosis.
5. *Conclude by submitting to your higher self any question*

you have about your life, decisions you are about to make, or future developments. State each question aloud and give thanks in advance for the answers you will get during your next session.

How a Securities Salesman Made a "Financial Killing" with Cosmosis

Mr. Blake was a securities salesman with a well-known brokerage firm. He dabbled occasionally in growth stocks, hoping to buy low and sell high within a short time.

He came to me for a reading and I suggested that we try the Cosmosis formula for mental power. Actually, his mind was so filled with ideas, possible purchases, that he was almost always "jammed up" mentally.

Blake used the formula, and *after only three sessions* he got an impression that he should purchase a little-known oil stock. He did so at a very low price. Two weeks later, that very same company struck a well that made their operations most profitable. He sold the stock and made a handsome profit.

But, it didn't end there. Today, he is one of the most successful men in his field and his personal fortune is an exceptionally large one.

How Joan Saved Her Romance with Cosmosis

Joan was a college student. Bright and beautiful, she was entirely in love with a boy who was confused and immature because of his dependence on drugs. They had discussed his problems and how it caused friction, misunderstanding, and resentment in their relationship.

They needed help from a power outside themselves. Their late-night "discussions" didn't help. Intellectually,

24

they knew that the problem was growing. But they were up against a wall when it came to finding a solution. Joan wanted her lover to stop taking drugs. He couldn't see the danger.

First Joan, herself, started using Cosmosis to clear her own thinking. She wanted new ways of dealing with the boy she loved because she knew they could be very happy together.

She found that she was looking at things differently. In fact, a dramatic change started to come over her. She was not resentful. She neutralized discussions that would have become arguments. She was actually more patient, and really loving.

Naturally, she told her boyfriend about her Cosmosis formula and the benefits she was receiving mentally and emotionally. She had more control over herself and her reactions.

He became interested enough to try it himself! That's when things really started to happen. He became a regular Cosmosis practitioner.

Slowly, he stopped using drugs as he found the inner peace and truth of his own individuality and divinity! They were both thankful. He returned to normal health as the natural balance took over in his mind and body.

Life is energy in motion. Cosmosis is the energy of the universe which is in you now. All it takes to focus and use this transforming power is the recognition that it is there and knowing the means for activating it. The magic Cosmosis formula presented in this chapter can help you lead a better life.

Psychic powers are there for the asking.

Each chapter of this book will give you the techniques and methods for dynamic living, Cosmosis-infused experiences that will amaze you and astound your friends.

POINTS TO REMEMBER FROM THIS CHAPTER

1. Cosmic rays, or solar energy, enter our lungs as we breathe and help to support the life force or Prana *within our bodies. These rays can be focused at the base of the spine for the awakening of* Kundalini *power.*

2. This Kundalini power rises along the spine to awaken the psychic centers. As it reaches the brain, it charges our thoughts and emotions with Cosmosis. As our thoughts and emotions are changed, the outer world, the world of experience, is attuned with Cosmosis and becomes rewarding and healthy.

3. Kundalini is awakened with the magic Cosmosis formula *of breathing regularly, holding the breath while the energy is visualized at the base of the spine, and exhaling naturally.*

26

Chapter 2

HOW TO UNDERSTAND THE PAST AND SEE INTO THE FUTURE WITH COSMOSIS

You can apply a few simple Cosmosis techniques to understand your past and see into your future! The psychic ability to do this is *clairvoyance.* Cosmosis activates the wavelength of your superconscious mind, *which knows all things* that are happening, have happened, or will happen.

Most of us are concerned with a place in *time* we call "now," and we certainly think of ourselves as being fixed in the physical *space* we occupy. In other words, we assume we are caught at a specific point in time and space. We are in a *time-space axis.*

Cosmosis gives us a mobility in time and space which is called *breaking the time-space axis.* This chapter will teach you how to *break the time axis* so you can go either forward or backward in time.

**How Pat Broke the Time Axis
to Avoid an Automobile Accident**

Pat Z. was planning a trip from Detroit to Chicago to

27

visit her mother. It's expressway all the way. And, although the weather was cool and clear, a pleasant summer day, she had a feeling of anxiety. You may have had the same kind of sensation yourself. Schooled in the psychic ways of Cosmosis, she knew it would be a good idea to meditate on the trip before she took it.

She visualized herself moving along the road and asked the question, "Should I make the trip to Chicago as planned?" She waited silently for the answer. Each time she got a negative feeling and a visual impression of cars in an accident.

Pat changed her question. Should she go at another time? In answer to this question she got an affirmative feeling, and she saw her car traveling over the expressway easily and safely. So she changed her departure to another day and was able to go without any accident.

While she was traveling, she saw a pileup of several cars along the road. The accident looked recent.

Was this the accident that Pat had seen in her vision? Were the twisted cars a reminder of what could have happened? Would her car have been in the lethal wreckage if she had made the trip a day or so earlier? No one knows for sure, but Pat was convinced that she had avoided just such a devastating accident because of the psychic power released by Cosmosis.

How James R. Broke the Time Axis to See a Former Existence

Do you ever wonder why you make some of the same mistakes over and over?

That thought occurred to James R., a senior executive with a large computer corporation.

His problem was women. In fact, he was into his third marriage when we met accidentally in a restaurant. We were having a late evening snack. I was reading a well-

28

known psychic book and he was looking through a newspaper.

"I see you are interested in psychic matters," he said, referring to my book.

"Yes, in fact I am a psychic practitioner," I responded.

We got into a discussion after that and I explained how the spiritual energy in the universe works.

"It seems awfully hard to depend on such an elusive thing as this Cosmosis business. I've always wondered about reincarnation, though. I'm about to get a third divorce and I wonder if a previous life is somehow making it impossible to have a happy marriage. I'm really bugged by it. Honestly, it seems as though I cannot find the right wife," he said.

"Cosmosis can activate your psychic power to read your own past. It may enable you to see a former life and relate it to this one. You might be under the influence of a Karmic debt," I concluded.

"A Karmic what?" he asked apologetically.

"Karma is an ancient Sanskrit word for the law of cause and effect. Everything you've ever done affects what happens to you today. That's the basic idea. Suppose you've done something in a previous life that is blocking your marriage? Until you know what it is and how to overcome the Karmic condition, you'll keep on having this trouble," I explained.

"Well, that does make sense," he answered, with a glint of hope in his voice.

We set an appointment, and he started to awaken the Kundalini force within his body. Finally, he started to unfold mentally and emotionally. Then, one night, he dreamed that he was a sultan in the Middle East.

He had a harem which displeased him because his wives made demands for better treatment, food, and living conditions. In a fit of rage he had them all executed.

He got to thinking about the dream, which was very

vivid. We discussed the entire matter at his next session and concluded together that this was a perfect explanation for his present condition. But if this was so, then we had the task of removing the condition. What could we do about that?

We puzzled about this matter for several days. Then we hit upon the idea of doing a good deed on a mass basis that might somehow make up for his destruction of these women in a previous life.

Jim hit upon the idea of helping a girls' orphanage financially. That was the beginning. He could afford to be generous. He made an initial contribution and after several months was asked to serve on the Board of Directors. His administrative ability helped enormously and the orphanage thrived.

Then something strange and beautiful happened. Real love and tender concern grew back into his marriage, and Jim decided not to get a divorce after all.

Coincidence? The hand of Fate? Karma overcome?

Maybe it was all three. One thing we could say for certain was that Cosmosis has a great way of helping people, regardless of their problem.

HOW COSMOSIS BREAKS
THE TIME-SPACE AXIS

Once alignment is made with Ultimate Reality, the superconscious mind is filled with Cosmic energies which lift the consciousness above fixed positions in time and space.

The key to Cosmic alignment with Ultimate Reality is to be free of ego-identity, or personal selfhood. We are not separated individualities, but are related to all of creation, all persons, all things. The same "force" which impels us

along life's pathway also permeates other forms of creation.

Cosmosis lifts our consciousness above the limits of our material sense and reason when we realize our common relationship to everything that exists. Then we are open to the natural ebb and flow of Cosmosis.

KNOW THE TRUE MEANING
OF YOUR PAST

What you do today affects what you *are* tomorrow.

Everything you say, think, or take action on today reverberates in your life tomorrow. Everything you experience in this life tends to affect your future existences. Thus, your past lives influence your present life.

Past lives leave a Cosmic trace which is carried over into your personality in this life. This trace, or Karma, can cause you to make the same mistakes over and over again unless you overcome the effects of these *inevitable influences* in your life. You may even find yourself repeating the same kinds of failures, disappointments, and frustrating experiences in the life you are leading now.

Cosmosis can enable you to tune in, through your superconscious mind, to the *Akashic Record*—the eternal imprint of everything that has happened. By "reading" these Akashic Records, you can see *how* your past lives may be influencing your present existence. Knowing this, you can proceed to *remove these influences and progress into a life free from mental, social, and spiritual tensions and pressures.*

If you are like most people you *also* have abilities, strong points, and *beneficial influences* from your past lives *which can aid you in the present,* once you know what they are and can accent their development.

31

THE TECHNIQUE FOR ATTUNEMENT
WITH THE AKASHIC RECORDS

Here is the method for making lasting attunement with the Akashic Records and for realizing, in the very depths of your being, what Cosmic lessons and Karmic conditions you have to live with in this life.

First, take a few deep breaths as you are seated in your meditation chair. Hold each breath for a few seconds. Exhale slowly and deeply. As you breathe, comfortable in this relaxed and deep way, *repel any conscious thoughts of yourself* or negative thoughts about your life. Simply let your mind think about your breathing. Send all conscious material away from you. See it going into the ocean, deep into a forest, or other neutral place.

Second, increase your relaxation, your mental inactivity.

Third, once you have adapted yourself to complete neutrality, complete receptivity, *ask this question out loud:* "Please show me the Akashic Records for myself. Let me know what I have to overcome and what progress I can make in this life to develop a positive Karmic reaction in my future unfoldment."

Once you have presented this petition, your superconscious mind will present various images or impressions which will give you the meanings which you are seeking.

Keep a small notebook in which you can record the impressions which you get. At first the signals may be weak or slightly distorted, and some of the direction you get may be symbolic. But stay with it and you will be given the fragments you need to build a more positive life.

**How Akashic Attunement Helped Mark
Find His Direction in Life**

Mark was a college student who had reached a personal revelation of staggering proportions. He was studying as a premedical student. He was doing well in his academic work but was uneasy in his personal conviction that he was following the right course for his life.

Naturally he was concerned, because he had been investing his time and effort working toward a specific end—entrance into medical school.

We spoke together about the technique for attunement with the Akashic Records. He tried it, and during his attunement he began to see a previous life as a medical doctor during the time of Ancient Egypt. He had healed people through the use of light rays reflected through jewels. He had been experimenting with the healing power of amber when his life was cut short by accidental drowning.

This record caused him to realize that he was being impelled to do medical work because of his disappointment over not being able to complete his experiments. He knew, too, that he didn't really want to be a medical doctor. His desire was simply the appearance of this Karmic trace from his previous life. What he really wanted to do was *help his fellow human beings.* This deep desire to serve others had motivated him originally to be a physician.

The realization of his true feeling about life opened up vast new possibilities to Mark. He could do many kinds of work and still be in a position to serve others. He actually reached the conclusion that he could serve others better by being a social worker. He discontinued his medical studies and started to work toward his degree in social work.

Today he is happier, at ease with himself, and delighted with the field he is in.

This is just *one* of many cases where knowledge of a previous life made a tremendous difference.

HOW TO READ YOUR FUTURE CLAIRVOYANTLY

Cosmosis can help you read your future clairvoyantly.

Cosmosis energy gives you the necessary *entrance point* into the time-space line.

Time and space are continuous. Often events cast their shadows in the present because *future events in your life are forming in the present.* Cosmic rays are entering our atmosphere all the time. As these rays energize your thoughts, the superconscious mind is released to move backward and forward along the time-space line. Cosmosis breaks the bounds of time and space, opens your clairvoyant vision, and presents you with the future event.

Here is the basic technique:

Cosmosis opens your "third eye" as the Kundalini power rises up the spine and radiates to a spot in the center of your forehead.

1. *Regular Breathing.* As you sit quietly in meditation, breathe at your regular rate, easily, comfortably. Be *aware* of your breathing and the pulsating of blood throughout your body. Notice the indwelling of the Cosmic energy as you breathe in.

2. *Hold Your Breath and Focus the Energy.* After you have taken air in, hold your breath a few seconds before you discharge the air. As you are holding your breath, see the building up of Cosmosis at the base of the spine.

3. *Directing Cosmosis into the Third Eye.* Focus and direct the energy up the spine and to a spot between your eyes, near the center of your forehead. You will feel the opening of the "third eye" of clairvoyance. Keep your physical eyes lightly closed. *Watch for impressions, mental images, and feelings.* Your clairvoyant ability will register as a "feeling" about something coming forward to you in time. You will get symbolic impressions and eventually you will see *very specific events taking place.*

Let your conscious activities be guided by these impressions. You may find that your logical, reasoning, conscious mind will try to argue you out of faith in these impressions. Don't let it! The mental feelings, hunches, and clairvoyant insight that you get will be more profitable, healthier, and truer than any amount of conscious, logical activity.

How Mary Failed to Follow Her
Cosmosis Impulse or Hunch

Mary was in a tight spot with respect to her work. She had been a secretary to a high-level executive for a large utility firm. She liked her work and was appreciated by her boss. Since she'd been doing the same work for about seven years, she had reached the highest point in her salary range. Yet, she felt the need for more money. She wanted an increase to help pay doctor bills for her ailing mother. Mary's third eye of clairvoyance had just begun to open. And, one night as she was directing the energy for guidance with respect to future events, she had a vision.

She was seated in her living room with a single lighted candle.

Suddenly she was given an impression of herself seated at another desk, in a new office, doing work other than that which she was actually doing in the present. It was just what she wanted, an answer to her every desire. But, no sooner had she received this vision than she started to think *consciously* about it.

She interpreted the vision to mean that she should look for another job—one that would pay more. But she was wrong, as she was about to learn in a few days.

Mary began to think about the proper way to look for another job. She went so far as to make application at several firms, and she was accepted by two other companies. She was trying to make up her mind about which offer to accept when it happened—she was shown how *wrong* her *conscious interpretation* had been.

35

Mary's boss called her in to give her the news. He was being promoted! Mary was to go along with him to the new job. She would get a new classification, be put into a new salary range, and get an immediate increase in pay.

Her dream had been fulfilled. Had Mary been satisfied to accept the vision as she got it, she would not have spent the time stewing and brewing, looking here and there, and going through all the fuss of applying elsewhere. It was her conscious mind, her logic, and her reason which led her astray.

"I'll be sure to let myself go with future impressions and not try to beat them into a logical framework," she said as she told me her story.

How Al Used Clairvoyance to Make the Right Connection

Al G. was a successful small businessman. He owned several dry cleaning establishments in a medium-sized Midwestern city.

"I'd like to reinvest my profits in something else, but I don't seem to be able to find the right thing," he said as we sat down in my study.

Al had a little more than $10,000 to invest in a business other than dry cleaning. We started with the magic Cosmosis formula. Al could visualize the energy moving up his spine and into the area of the third eye.

He was practicing the technique one evening in his office. It was late and he was about to go home.

Suddenly a number began to form in his mind's eye. First one digit—then, two digits—three—finally, seven numbers came in. It looked like an address. No, he reasoned, it was a telephone number. But whose number was it?

He decided to sleep on it. The next morning he called the number only to find the office of an attorney.

"Are you calling with respect to the newspaper ad?" a

36

pleasant female voice asked.

"I guess so," he replied, before he had a chance to explain.

Quickly the girl switched him to a man who began telling him *about an investment opportunity in a ski resort.* The backers of the project needed another $10,000 and were willing to give a partnership to the person with the money to put up.

That was it! Al invested in a ski resort and has tripled the value of his original investment.

SEEING MAJOR NEWS EVENTS
BEFORE THEY HAPPEN

If you are using the Cosmosis technique regularly, you will tune into world events before they actually take place. Such famous psychic personalities as Jean Dixon, Arthur Ford, Harold Sherman, Peter Hurkos, and others have frequently received visions of events of great historical significance before they've taken place. Even the wonderful British medium, Eileen Garett, sees things before they occur.

You can develop this same ability!

Here is a simple way to move easily out of the time-space axis of the "now" moment and place yourself ahead of time to sense psychically that which is going to happen.

Take a current newspaper or newsmagazine. Quickly flip through the pages until your eye naturally falls on a story which interests you.

Go into a silent meditation, free from distractions, and relax. Let your mind casually think about the news story. Use the following affirmation to capture and direct the Cosmosis wavelength to work for you: "Cosmosis energy, show me the meaning of this news event."

You will receive the Cosmic interpretation of the event

37

and you may also be shown additional events related to this one. If you are like most people who have invoked Cosmosis, you will be able to perceive other happenings yet to come, which are related in a deep, psychic way with the original news story.

CREATING FUTURE EVENTS
BY COSMOSIS VISUALIZATION

Now you are ready for the most fascinating demonstration of psychic power. *You are ready to use Cosmosis to create future events.*

The power behind psychic visualization is Cosmosis. Manifesting an event is easy when you know this technique. Bear in mind that all events are continuous. One thing leads to another. One event causes a result which acts and reacts to create other events. *Nothing that happens* on this plane of awareness, the earth plane, *happens independently.* Everything is related to other *causal factors.*

Now you have the secret of using Cosmosis to bring about an event in the future for your benefit. A psychic link or opening is needed to induce the desired event. When the "psychic opening" is made, you dynamically employ Cosmosis power to manifest the result.

In occult and mystical traditions, the technique of psychic visualization is called the "link-target-result" method.

You'll need a link or psychic opening to the event you are going to manifest. Cosmosis needs this contact point with the person or persons or situation which you want to activate. In other words, Cosmosis needs a method of transmitting itself, a channel through which it can travel. A photograph of the person, an object closely associated with the place to be influenced, or anything which you have designated as a symbolic "stand-in" for the event will work.

Here are some examples of the "stand-in" . . . money is an obvious stand-in for wealth . . . a healthy, growing plant is an excellent stand-in symbol for better health . . . soil can be made to represent property . . . a photograph of a person can be a stand-in for that person.

The link to the event secretly opens the door for Cosmosis to change the causative factors in your favor. *It is all done by indirection.*

HOW TO DECIDE ON THE PROPER LINK
OR PSYCHIC OPENING

After meditating briefly, select your link according to your own intuition. What seems right? Go by your feelings rather than by logic or conscious decision.

Once you've selected your link to the event (target), you are ready to invoke Cosmosis.

Set aside a quiet time in a place where you will not be interrupted until you have finished the invocation ritual, which is based on the ancient wisdom teachings of the Egyptians. Night is best but you can perform this rite during the day. No one but you—or your fellow practitioners—should be present. Don't allow curiosity seekers to observe your ritual.

THE RITUAL FOR CREATING FUTURE EVENTS
WITH COSMOSIS

Place a clean cloth on a small table. Silently light a single candle which stands for the one power in the universe. Recite the following incantation: "One force, one power, one universal energy, we call upon the Eternal One to enter these proceedings."

Visualize the Cosmic forces entering the room.

Breathe deeply and rhythmically as the forces gather.

You do not need to hold your breath or focus the energy. You are not taking the Cosmosis into your body. You want it to move into your actions and into the link. Then recite the following out loud: "We are representing this object *(hold the object up)* as the channel through which the one power can flow to activate *(name the event or situation that you want to have manifested)."*

Repeat this action three times. Extend your thanks: "We give thanks for all that is given to us."

Extinguish the candle and place the object in a safe place, where no one will see it, touch it, or disturb it in any way.

This object must be kept safe until the event has taken place. Then it can be deactivated with the same ritual.

Repeat this ritual each day, until the event or situation has materialized.

This ancient ritual has been used to:

* Multiply financial and business success.
* Bring harmonious personal relationships into being.
* Draw a loved one back after a violent argument.
* Repel a dangerous enemy.
* Gain a promotion to a better job.
* Control a family member who was causing trouble.
* Create tremendous popularity with friends.

HOW TO DEACTIVATE YOUR PSYCHIC LINK

After the event has taken place, light your candle and place the object on a clean cloth.

Begin by giving thanks, three times: "We give thanks for all that was given to us."

Deactivate your object by holding it up and saying: "One force, one power, one universal energy, we call upon the Eternal One to withdraw the power from this object. This is no longer the link to *(name the event)*."

How Jess Influenced His Future Wife

Jess D. was a man obsessed with finding the right woman to marry. A widower at an early age, he had a successful building contractor business. Jess was the father of two girls from his first marriage and he wanted to marry again. But, he wanted to find the most loving, dedicated woman possible to raise his girls and form a happy life with him. It was a beautiful desire, and we taught him the Cosmosis method of creating the event ahead of time.

Jess made fantastic use of the ritual.

He bought an inexpensive woman's wedding ring as the link to his future wife. He only wanted to be led, somehow, to the right wife.

Three months after he used this ritual, he accidentally met an airline stewardess at a drugstore soda fountain. Three months after that meeting he was married to her, happily.

How Elizabeth Used the Ritual
on a Neighbor

Elizabeth lived in a suburb of a large city. She was alone and unmarried in a small, well-kept frame house. Her recreation in the summer consisted of gardening. She was raising award-winning roses.

The problem she had may sound small to some, but to her—with her love and concern for her roses—it was shattering.

Elizabeth had neighbors who owned two boxer dogs that were left to roam at will. Frequently, they came into Elizabeth's garden and damaged her prize rose bushes.

41

She used one of the damaged rose branches as her link to the dogs and to their owner. Many times she had mentioned the dogs' intrusion on her property, but the neighbors still let them loose. It was against the local ordinance to let the dogs run wild. Elizabeth used the ritual, since her appeals to reasonable action and restraint had fallen on deaf ears.

Without warning of any kind only a few days after she used the ritual, *only one time,* the neighbors installed a special fenced-in area for the dogs to run in.

Cheerfully and with a little extra wink in her eye, Elizabeth reported to me what had happened. She was pleased and the old enthusiasm and sparkle had returned to her.

How Fred Used the Ritual
on His Supervisor

Fred worked in a steel mill for a very difficult supervisor. As soon as Fred finished a job, there was "the man" again with something to complain about or another job to do.

One day Fred was called into the office and told that his work was not up to par. The reasons given were vague but he knew he had to do something to salvage his reputation and keep his job.

Fred realized that if he acted out of panic or thought of himself as persecuted, he would probably do the wrong things and his fate would be sealed. He might be fired or transferred to another job, where his chances for advancement would be nil.

He resolved to do the best he could—no matter what happened.

Knowing full well how things can fall in on a person

42

under tension and pressure, Fred decided to perform the ritual on his supervisor. He asked that the supervisor see him objectively, evaluate his work honestly, and give him the benefit of the doubt.

The psychic link to the supervisor was Fred's paycheck stub—a fitting symbol indeed.

Within a month—Fred used the ritual each day—another meeting was held. Things were looking better for Fred.

Two months later, he had a clean record and he was back in the running for a pay raise. Fred thanked his lucky stars *and* the simple ritual I taught him through Cosmosis.

THE RELATIVE NATURE
OF TIME AND SPACE

Time and space are relative. They are continuous parts of an ongoing evolutionary process. You can use the techniques outlined here to pull yourself out of a fixed position, mold your future, understand your past mistakes, and capitalize on everything that you do.

Once you transcend the false idea that you are limited by time or space, your life can take on new meaning. You will be in command of your own destiny because you will be able to guide your actions and reactions in the present.

Nothing in this world is really beyond your grasp when you use the Universal Power of Cosmosis. The methods for activating this energy are simple, and the fascinating stories of those who have mastered this art are living proof that you, too, can live a life of beauty, splendor, and wealth.

Try overcoming time and space. Then go on to the next chapter where another step in your trip to a better life is waiting for you.

Points to Remember from This Chapter

1. Cosmosis works with your superconscious mind to give you the gift of clairvoyance and the ability to break the time-space axis.

2. Understanding your past is just as important as seeing the future.

3. Past lives can be revealed as memory traces on the Akashic Records.

4. A psychic entrance point is needed to foretell future happenings.

5. With a link to a future event, you can create its manifestation with Cosmosis.

Chapter 3

HOW COSMOSIS PUTS YOU AT THE RIGHT PLACE FOR YOUR BEST ADVANTAGE

You are about to see how Cosmosis can give you the key to the true intentions of other people and how it places *you* at the *right place* to take advantage of opportunities.

The ability to send and receive thoughts—to understand the *entire* truth of situations—is the subject of this chapter.

You'll also learn how to control and motivate people, how to know when you are being *told* the truth, and how to know *what* the people around you are planning to do.

HOW TO MAKE TELEPATHIC ATTUNEMENT WITH THOUGHT-FORMS

All things in the universe are in "vibration." Matter is made up of tiny *moving* particles. The speed with which these particles are moving is the "frequency" of their vibration.

Thoughts do not die. They live on in the frequency of their thought-forms.

Cosmosis enlivens the extrasensory capacities of the superconscious mind. Your superconscious makes contact with the thought-forms of other people.

Following is the technique for reading thought-forms of others:

1. *Meditational Repose.* Place yourself in a quiet, relaxed position in an upright chair. Be free from distractions or interruptions.

2. *Mentally Attune.* After you have put aside conscious thought about the day's activity, slowly bring to mind the person or situation with which you want to attune.

3. *Receive the Impressions.* Keep a writing tablet beside you, and as you get impressions from the person or situation, mark them down for reference later.

4. *Make Additional Attunements.* Sit again at a later time to get additional impressions and to verify the first sitting.

5. *Coordinate the Information You Get.* Once you have collected sufficient data on your writing tablet, you are ready for conscious, logical interpretation of the impressions—many of which may be symbolic. Think of the data as a puzzle which you are putting together for the very first time.

The meaning of the thought-forms you have gathered will become apparent to you quickly. Disregard any tendency to "second-guess" yourself, and do not take into consideration any thought-forms which are vague and indefinite. Indefinite forms are still in a state of formation. Future sittings will bring these matters into clearer perspective.

Shirley N. was an excellent copywriter for a large advertising agency. She was using this technique to attune with friends of hers, mostly artists and writers, in another city. She picked up impressions from their thought-forms which indicated that several of them were in the process of working on a lucrative, new advertising project.

She telephoned one of these friends to confirm her impressions.

"We're so glad you called," said Alice R. "We are working on a special project commissioned by a governmental agency. It is a traveling display and we need someone to write copy for the brochure which will accompany it. We need descriptive information to be written for each exhibit, but everyone here is tied up. Could you do it? The assignment pays $1,000."

Shirley jumped at the chance to do the work and earn an extra $1,000.

Everything worked perfectly through following the program outlined previously. She got the background information and the details by mail. She was able to write the copy in her spare time, and the agency that commissioned the project was delighted with her work. The money came in handy, too, because she used it as tuition for some evening classes she was taking toward her master's degree in journalism.

How Walter Attracted Enough Votes to Become County Clerk

Walter was running on his party's ticket for county clerk in a small county of Ohio. Instead of using the technique to tune into the thoughts of others, he reversed the process and *sent* thoughts to influence voters.

He placed himself in meditational repose and made the mental attunement (step # 1 and 2 of the program set out previously). Then he sent out a strong thought in the form of an affirmation: He concentrated on the idea that he would do his best, and asked for voter support.

The affirmation he repeated over and over in his mind

47

was: "I will do my best to serve you as county clerk. Please vote for me."

Walter won the election.

But the best part of his story is that he only had to spend about 15 minutes a day doing this. Once he had broadcast the thought of his great desire, he let go of the situation and let Cosmosis work for him. That was the real secret of his success. *He did not force the outcome,* but rather, let Cosmosis create the favorable vote for him.

HOW TO MULTIPLY YOUR POWER
OF PSYCHIC ATTRACTION

Your overall power to attract favorable opportunities and place yourself where you can take advantage of them can be increased by Cosmosis.

Here is how you can broadcast a thought-form and influence other people:

1. Establish who you want to influence, and exactly how you expect that influence to affect the person. Make sure there will not be adverse results from this effort, as side effects can often backfire and reverse the condition you are hoping to establish.

2. Put your mind in meditational repose. Be relaxed and free from distracting ideas.

3. Call to mind the person you want to influence and the action you expect that person to take. Breathe evenly and deeply. As you feel the Cosmic energy entering your lungs, repeat the thought in your mind. See the thought-form going out to the person or persons you are influencing.

4. See favorable circumstances around you; picture many kinds of opportunities. Let your imagination run un-

48

restricted. Don't stop with the little things—think big. Visualize obtaining what you want. See yourself doing, being, or having the ideal life in every way. Open every channel of opportunity in visualizing the objects of your desires.

5. Rest, put your thoughts into "neutral." Release all concentration. Stop visualizing.

6. Affirm that you will be attracted to the right circumstances, at the right time, to take advantage of every opportunity. Use an affirmation similar to the following one:

"I am attracting only good, beneficial circumstances to me. Every aspect of my life is open to opportunity. The power of psychic attraction is multiplying within me and around me."

How Jean Got a Transfer and a Promotion

Jean was a long-distance telephone operator. She wanted a transfer to another city to be near her ailing mother.

She put in her request for transfer with her supervisor and used the Cosmosis method to increase her psychic attraction and put herself into the right job.

It was well known that openings in the city where her mother lived were not frequent.

After several months of waiting, she called me and said, "I still haven't heard anything. Not even a hint. I have no idea what's going to happen. Maybe it is a lost cause for me. I feel so sorry for my mother who is all alone."

We spent a few minutes meditating over the telephone together. Although we got a positive feeling after we meditated, we didn't get any impressions as to the outcome of her request.

49

It happened the next day. Without any warning, her supervisor called her in and said word had arrived that a transfer was possible . . . if.

"We have approval for your transfer *if* you are willing to accept a promotion to service assistant. Your evaluations show you are ready for more responsibility and we'd like to give it to you," her chief operator told her.

"I'm delighted to accept," Jean said.

Jean certainly was at the *right place* at the *right time* when she decided to put in her request for a transfer.

How Nancy Gained Peace of Mind with Psychic Attraction

Nancy D. started a happy, worthwhile, satisfying life when she applied psychic attraction through Cosmosis.

"I just can't sleep at night. Sometimes I toss and turn until three or four in the morning. Then I wake up exhausted; I can hardly last the day at work," she explained to me.

"Is there anything troubling you?" I asked.

"That's just it. Maybe I shouldn't watch the news on television before I go to bed. I don't have any troubles. I just can't put my finger on it," Nancy answered.

Today's way of living creates strain. There are hidden pressures, a feeling that a crisis may lurk around the next corner. These insecurities sometimes build themselves into a vast subconscious terror. This fear of the unknown can cause insomnia, inability to sleep.

"A change in mental attitude is the secret to peace of mind. But, sometimes we need more than the realization that positive thinking can make the difference. You may need the spiritual power of the universe, Cosmosis, to help make a lasting change," I said.

Nancy started her therapy with the magic Cosmosis

formula you are now familiar with, the breathing exercises for activating the Kundalini force in her body and mind.

Coupled with the magic Cosmosis formula, Nancy's program for self-improvement included psychic attraction. She pictured herself being surrounded by tranquil scenes. She visualized herself by a quiet lake, near a beautiful seashore, high on a cool mountain. She was actually influencing her subconscious mind with these counter-thoughts further activated by Cosmosis.

Nancy and I always prayed together, too. We simply turned the matter over to God and asked for help. We knew that in some mysterious way God was part of this wonderful Cosmosis force.

The demonstration started a little at a time. First Nancy was able to get to sleep a half-hour or an hour earlier than usual. By the time Nancy could feel the Kundalini in her head, she was more relaxed and at ease in her job.

The unnamed fear and anxiety left Nancy's life completely. It was a real miracle. She could rest, relax, and sleep normally. The renewing strength of a full night's sleep gave her the pep and vitality she needed to tackle any challenge.

More happened. Nancy's personality became more outgoing, more understanding. People seemed to gravitate toward her. She seemed to give off a vibration that was beautiful and appealing because her calmness was delightfully "catching."

How Walton's Eye Disease Was Cured

Walton S. was a member of our church who had studied metaphysical matters for his entire lifetime.

He followed closely the healings in the ministry of Katherine Kuhlman and in Christian Science. He was not opposed to conventional medical practice but he was

51

enthusiastic about spiritual healing. Now he had a healing crisis of his own. His vision blurred unexpectedly.

He had an eye condition that defied both medical treatment and spiritual healing.

Walton used psychic attraction to find the proper medical specialist. He broadcast the thought each night that he be placed with the right doctor.

His own family physician recommended a doctor in Canada who used a new cure.

Walton now sees without hindrance, thanks to being guided to the right doctor.

HOW TO CONTROL AND MOTIVATE PEOPLE

Getting along with people is not the key to motivating and controlling their actions. If you are popular, it helps. But being a pleasant person or "good guy" is not leadership.

People will follow your lead when they realize two things. First, they must recognize that you are distinctive, unique—an individualist. Second, they must recognize that you have power which they can share by following your lead.

Almost every leader you can think of has these two qualities.

People you meet should sense your independence and power immediately if you've been using Cosmosis. Their attention should be drawn to you and to you alone. You must begin your control of their actions by attracting and controlling their attention. If people pay no attention to you, they cannot be motivated by your suggestions. That's obvious. But how?

You must build an image of yourself as a power *even before people get to know you.* You must say things, do things, which make you a legend. But don't be afraid to make a few enemies. The object is not to get everyone to like you. Your objective is to build the kind of image and develop a personal strategy which will enable you to control and dominate *some* people. Your empire does not need to be the whole world. But it does need to include your *part* of the world—which cannot be disputed.

What is there about you which can set you apart from others?

Remember that your power begins with your distinctiveness. You do not want to be part of a class, group, or segment of society. So, your individuality must be clearly visible.

A CHECKLIST FOR INDIVIDUALITY AND IMAGE-BUILDING

You do not have to adopt the methods of others to be different. You do not have to assume a new role or act your way to power. You can gain the appearance of success and individuality by emphasizing the interesting personality that you already have. Here is a checklist of questions which can help you decide what to make people notice about you. You want to stand out in a crowd as someone who *has something that other people want or need.* You don't want to appear absurd or uncomfortable. That is why you should only emphasize what you've already got going for you.

1. *Start with Your Appearance.* What would you really like to wear? Why not wear it? Don't be persuaded to be conservative. Be yourself and select your clothes based on what appeals to you.
2. *Take Your Interests Next.* Most really influential people

53

have several hobbies and interests which seem almost contradictory. Take the subjects which you might enjoy and find out about them. Do you like space travel? Wine making? Music? Art? Gardening? French poodles? Politics? The stock market? Interior design? Any of these can get you started. Why? Because everyone likes to get "inside information" on subjects in which they are not well versed.

Anyone will listen to what you have to say about the things you are interested in if: (a) you know what you are talking about, and (b) you make the subject interesting. Don't boast about your knowledge. Tell it as though you were just chatting about a news item. An opening gambit might go like this: "Say Frank, did you know that the Dow-Jones Industrial average has never gone above 1, 000?" Or try "Mary, did you know that you could make wine in your own home in only three weeks; it only costs 55 cents for a gallon of excellent port." Most people will give you a hearing.

3. *Remake Your Attitude About Yourself.* No one will follow you if you are uncertain about what you say or if you leave the door open for failure. Of course, nothing succeeds like success. Your attitude telegraphs itself to people. Enthusiasm, pride, confidence, and joy are marks of a good attitude. Rule out depression, negative approaches, sadness, and self-examination. You will be as likely to be victimized by bad habits as anyone else. Just don't let them show. Be ready for challenge. You are ahead of everyone and everything. You are the master of your own destiny. Nothing can stop you from being *the* person in the lives of those near you.

4. *Beam in on Everyone and Everything.* A leader knows what's going on. He has more than his share of curiosity. He wants to keep his finger on the pulse of things. Because of this, he gives every person and every group the impression that they have his undivided attention.

See, hear, and feel everything that is going on around you. Don't ever be preoccupied when you are with people. Be alive and living in the present. When you show this keen desire to *know* and *be* with people, they will respond by being interested in you in the same way. Leadership is a two-way street. Give your attention and expect it from others. Stay beamed in every moment you are awake. Look people in the eye. Twinkle at them!

5. *Show People How to Meet Their Needs.* People will follow you if you can promise to meet their needs. They will listen to you if you can give them something. In turn, they will give you their loyalty. But, you must provide more than is expected. In other words, your followers must be led to think they are gaining more than they are giving. You'll be surprised to know that the more you give, the more you will receive. There is no end to the potential leadership you can have.

All people can be motivated to do something *if the doing of it meets a definite need.*

All people can be *controlled* as they do that something when they *see* real progress toward the fulfilling of that *need.*

You must remind people of their progress and help them farther along the road to their fulfilled needs.

Not all people have the same needs. Your perceptiveness, your ability to find each person's secret desire or unfulfilled wish, will carry you to a position of leadership. Find out what the other fellow wants. Then give it to him or show him how to get it. Some people want recognition; some desire money; others need love. Whatever it is, *you can make your control part of their motivation.*

Cosmosis gives you an extra lift in motivating other people because you are simply encouraging the Infinite Plan to unfold for each person you motivate.

UNFOLDING THE INFINITE PLAN THROUGH YOUR LEADERSHIP

So far we've explained what you can do when you are with people. Now here's the real, mystical secret to control over others.

Here is what you can do when you are *alone* that will enlist the unfailing support of the Cosmic tide of events, the Infinite Plan.

There is order behind all things in the universe. God's invisible design moves the tides predictably, the seasons on schedule. Even birth and death operate according to a master blueprint. We are evolving, growing, expressing all of the time. As you are able to show others how the Infinite Plan is working through all of life's experience, you will unlock the Cosmic chain of events to the happiness which they are seeking. No one wants to be at odds with the natural order of things, and no one needs to be. You can show how all of life, every happening, every change, is a building block to the *individual* expression of the Infinite Plan. Nothing is an accident. Everything leads to a greater good, to a clearer understanding of our true nature as infinite expressions of an Infinite Being.

With the dangers of earth existence multiplying all around us, human survival has become a major concern. If your leadership is itself controlled and directed by the higher forces represented by Cosmosis, you will be showing people not only how to meet their needs, but how, also, to survive mentally, emotionally, physically, and spiritually.

By dedicating your efforts to sincerely trying to help people, you will be a link in the Infinite Plan of human survival. Power for power's sake can only lead to destruc-

56

tion, but power assumed and cultivated for the unfoldment of God's Plan is unlimited since the plan itself is limitless.

How Leaders Were Developed
from Followers

Leaders throughout history have applied these steps to control and motivate their followers. Here are some case histories which are typical of hundreds in my files. Each individual has used the steps I've revealed here.

Carl M., a sales manager for a direct-selling cosmetic company, used these techniques with his salespeople and doubled his income in a year and one-half.

Mrs. W. S. employed these techniques in her job as a high school administrator. She found that the teachers under her jurisdiction were happier, taught their students more, and responded to her direction. Prior to her use of this method she had faculty morale problems, students and parents complained.

Mr. W. M. *failed* in his first attempt to apply these ideas because he didn't change his *attitude about himself*. He tried to apply the superficial signs of success but he didn't really think of himself as a leader. Mr. W. M. was an inner-city resident and captain of his block club. The residents in his neighborhood were trying to get the city to make some improvements. They needed better street lighting, faster refuse removal, and frequent street cleaning. Mr. W. M. couldn't get his block club to agree on a plan that would force the city to act. He had several good suggestions himself that would pressure the officials in charge. Each resident had his own suggestion and no one really wanted to follow his lead.

Things changed when Mr. W. M. started to force himself to be positive, confident, cheerful, no matter what took place. His show of cool confidence convinced himself and the other members of the club. The turning point came when they were at a standstill during one of their weekly meetings. They turned to him and asked for his suggestion. He outlined a plan he had been thinking about.

The plan was accepted enthusiastically, and Mr. W. M. helped organize the citizens to execute it. He literally turned his own failure in leadership into a pleasant, easily understood motivating factor which other people responded to quite readily.

He directed the plan he had suggested and the club succeeded in getting the attention and improvements which it wanted.

HOW TO MAKE DECISIONS
WHICH ARE RIGHT 90 PER CENT
OF THE TIME

Being at the right place at the right time to take advantage of the opportunity that is unfolding means that you've got to make decisions that are right.

Cosmosis can help you to be right most of the time.

Be sure to practice the Kundalini exercise in Chapter 1. This is an excellent preparation for using Cosmosis in decision making.

Right decisions are not made by your conscious mind. They are made by your "etheric self" or "oversoul," the spiritual double, which surrounds your body. Each of us has this etheric double which is an exact spiritual duplicate of the physical body.

Attunement with the etheric self or higher self guarantees access to the vast understanding that only comes from a source beyond the physical.

KING CONTACT WITH THE ETHERIC DOUBLE
FOR RIGHT DECISIONS

Creation is in your etheric self. It is simply moving at a higher rate of vibration. New paths to a life brimming with vitality and satisfaction are born in the higher realms, in the higher frequencies. Our own atomic structure was born by this higher intelligence. We call this intelligence Mother Nature or God. Yet, we all contain a portion of this creative power which manifests in the etheric.

The etheric self projects a magnetic force field and is sometimes seen by psychic people as an aura of color around a person's head. Often it is seen around the entire body. Once you know that a decision is called for, follow these steps:

1. *Assemble All the Information You Can.* Before leaping into a decision that you might have to live with for a long time, stop. Stop and gather all the data; find out all you can, every detail. Get more information about the situation than you think you'll need.

   This is an action of conscious mind. You'll find yourself trying logically to reach a conclusion, too. Don't! Just find out all you can. Check and double-check to make certain you've investigated all of the angles. Make a game out of it. Pretend you are a private detective looking for hidden clues. You'll be surprised to find how one single fact can make a difference in your future happiness.

2. *Decide on an Ultimate Goal.* Once you've gathered the facts, set them aside for the time being and decide on your ultimate goal. What do you want your decision to do for you? Where do you want to be after some time has elapsed? What do you expect to happen? You can be as imaginative in your thinking as you like. Think high, wide,

59

and handsome. Don't think small. Don't think about the present. Set your sights on the future.

3. *Once You've Set Your Ultimate Goal, Break It Down into Smaller Goals.* This is the key to decision making on the conscious level. What are the small goals, the little steps, which lead to the ultimate goal? What are the reasonable things you can do—over an extended period of time—which would lead to the ultimate goal? What are the ingredients of the ultimate goal?

Now you are ready to use your etheric double to help you make a decision—acted upon in the present—which will speed you toward the ultimate goal.

4. *Write the Decision on a Clean Paper.* Prepare the decision in the form of a question—for example: Should I buy this house? Should I change jobs? Will I be happy in this marriage? Is this investment wise? Should I move to another city? Is the person I am dating right for me? Should I get a divorce? What should I do now?

5. *Sit in Silence and Read the Question to Yourself for Several Minutes.*

6. *Visualize the Etheric Double Hearing the Question.* See an exact duplicate of your physical self. See this spiritual body around you or standing in front of you. Direct the question to this higher self and wait for the inner prompting that tells you the answer.

7. *Act on the Prompting Which You Get.* When you get the answer from your etheric double, act right away before your conscious mind has a chance to argue you out of the decision. Don't hesitate. Don't let logic interrupt you.

Each time you have a decision to make, use this technique. Take action as soon as possible. Recognize the need for a decision early—before a crisis develops—so you are in command of the way conditions evolve. Try not to place yourself in a position of responding to first one crisis and then another. Act before the emergency develops. Cosmosis will put you in the right place. Your etheric double will give you the right course of action.

HOW THE ETHERIC DOUBLE WILL LEAD YOU
TO SAY THE RIGHT THING

Decide to act—then act! What should you say? How should you act to take advantage of the opportunity?

Thinking about what you are going to say is not enough, because often a conversational situation develops spontaneously and you are likely to be caught without a script. If you are going to talk to your boss about a raise and you plan your "part" too much in advance, you might find yourself caught short suddenly when he says something you had not counted on. If you plan to raise the issue of marriage with your loved one and something unexpected happens, you could be thrown off the track.

The etheric double can act as a soothing, calming, directive agent when you are in tight spots, *when what you say affects your future as much as what you do.*

While you are sitting in visualization of the etheric double, repeat the thought that you will be led by its direction when you are in a critical meeting. You do not need to force the thought. Just quietly and firmly assert that you will be led by the double, not by your own fears, worries, frustrations, or conscious conclusions.

When pressure is on, visualize the etheric double, wait a second or two, and then say what you are led to say by it. Don't add to what you are being directed to say. Don't subtract from it. Tell it like it is, the way your higher self sees it. Call a spade a spade if you are directed to. Gloss over a personal insult if you are prompted to do so. When it gets down to the brass tacks of any tight spot, you *can* triumph.

POINTS TO REMEMBER FROM THIS CHAPTER

1. All things, people, places, and conditions in

61

the universe are in vibration. The speed of vibration is its frequency. Thoughts are in a higher rate of vibration than matter. Cosmosis enlivens our extrasensory facility of the superconscious mind so we can attune to the thought-forms of other people.

2. By broadcasting a thought-form, you can influence other people.

3. Controlling and motivating people depends on your leadership image. This individual image is built upon your appearance, your unique interests, your attitude about yourself, your "beam-in" ability, and your willingness to show people how to meet their needs. When you help people unfold the Infinite Plan in their lives, you are an inspired, master leader.

4. The "etheric double," your higher self, can help you make right decisions 90 per cent of the time.

5. When you are in a tight spot and the pressure is on to say the right thing, you can visualize the etheric double and let yourself be guided by it.

Chapter 4

HOW COSMOSIS MAKES EVERYTHING
YOU DO BECOME POSITIVE

There is one source of Cosmic power, but this power manifests itself in both positive and negative forms. This power is manifesting in your life right this minute. But you and I are not alone. All living things are composed of positive and negative electrical charges. In fact, the story of our universe is a story of the arrangement and rearrangement of matter which is both positive and negative.

This chapter will show you how Cosmosis can be the force which puts your life on a positive wavelength. *It will show you how to manifest positive results, no matter what you undertake to do.* Think of it. You have this power at your command right at this moment. This power can bring every desire into being. Let's see how it works.

This formula explains how to manifest your desires positively:

$$\underline{\text{STRONG}\atop\text{DESIRE}} + \underline{\text{ENOUGH}\atop\text{SPACE}} + \text{COSMOSIS} = \underline{\text{MANIFESTED}\atop\text{DESIRE}}$$

Strong desire creates a link with Cosmosis. This, in turn, releases the creative force of the universe for the manifestation of the desired happening.

Let's look at this a little more closely.

No person lives alone or in a vacuum. Eliminating anything from our life experience automatically creates "space" which is filled with new experience. There is only so much energy, so much time, only so much emotional and mental room for the fulfillment of our desires.

By taking a personal inventory, we make room for Cosmosis to work for us.

YOUR PERSONAL INVENTORY

Before we go further with the use of Cosmosis, take a pencil or pen, right now, and answer these simple questions. Let's see where you are and where you would like to go with your life. Analyze yourself by answering the following questions frankly and deliberately:

A. *What You Have Now*

1. How would you describe your home? Do you like it?

_____

2. What is your job or occupation? Do you like it?

_____

3. What is your financial status? Do you like it?

_____

4. How is your marriage working? Can it be improved?

_____

5. How are you getting along with friends and family?

———————————————————————

6. How is your health? Can it be improved?

———————————————————————

7. Is there anything you would like to do or have which you just can't seem to fit in?

———————————————————————

B. Changes You'd Like to Make

1. What changes would you like to make in your home?

———————————————————————

2. What would make your work more interesting to you?

———————————————————————

3. What changes in your marriage would make it happier?

———————————————————————

4. What financial alteration would make you more secure?

———————————————————————

5. What would improve your relations to family and friends?

———————————————————————

6. Would you like to improve your health and energy level?

———————————————————————

7. What would you really like to do with your life?

_____

C. *Setting Your Goals for the Future*

Where would you like to be five years from now with respect to each of the following? What would you like to have or be at that time?

1. Your home? _____
2. Your job? _____
3. Your finances? _____
4. Your marriage? _____
5. Your relations to family and friends? _____
6. Your health? _____
7. Your cherished dream or desire? _____

CREATING PSYCHIC SPACE
FOR CHANGE IN YOUR LIFE

Now you are ready to take the first steps toward the realization of your desires. You are about to clear the obstacles, the wasted time and energy, the frustrating experiences *to make way for dynamic Cosmosis action.* I am going to show you how to make enough psychic space to make way for the manifestation of your desires *in every aspec of your life.*

First, let's see how others have made way for dramatic change—even under the most adverse circumstances.

How Susan Made Room for Her Desire

Susan, like so many people, had filed for divorce from her husband of five years. She explained to me that they were no longer suited for each other. Possibly they never were.

As time for the final legal proceedings drew closer, she began to feel panic-stricken.

"It's not my guilt or even a feeling of fear," she explained. "I don't feel that my entire life has been a failure because of this divorce. What bothers me is what I'll do with my time alone. It's the prospect of loneliness that bothers me more than anything else."

She was having sleepless nights, fidgety days, and depressing thoughts.

What Susan was saying was that she was faced— possibly for the first time in her life—with genuine space, enough time to do whatever she wanted to do. You can see that up to this moment she had been busy doing the hundred-and-one things which every wife must do.

Now, all of a sudden, with the marriage coming apart, she was meeting her own negative feelings and emotions surrounding it. Yet, deep down inside, she knew also that she had a clear road ahead. She had the psychic space to step back and let Cosmosis bring her desire into being. But, what desire should she choose?

She had always wanted to own a small gift shop. To some people that may not seem like a very big desire. But to her it was "out of this world." It was an ideal which she had dreamed of many, many times. She had a natural, outgoing personality and loved to be with friends and acquaintances. A gift shop would give her two things. It would give her financial independence and a way to be close to people.

Susan set her mind to it, took her savings, found just the right location and got started. She hit the jackpot right away! People thronged to her shop. They loved her and the merchandise she chose to sell.

Today, Susan is happy, healthy, and quite successful. She now owns three shops in suburban locations, and they are all doing quite well.

The point of this story is that circumstances forced Susan to find something to fill the empty space in her life. She was goal oriented enough to capitalize on her vacant time, energy, and thought. Then, when she let go and allowed Cosmosis to carry her to her desired goal, she moved effortlessly and smoothly. It is true that she worked constructively and purposefully to realize her desire. But, she also had the secret weapon of that universal creative power, Cosmosis, working for her. During her quiet moments she tuned into that power, as outlined in Chapter 1, and then focused it on her desire. She brought that desire into being automatically, because she had these unseen energies of Cosmosis reaching out to bring her thought-forms into reality.

It is a good idea for you, too, to get rid of the extra baggage in your life in order to make room for the realization of your secret desire.

How John Forced Out Failure and Made Room for Success

John W., an insurance salesman in his early thirties, took the initiative to make sweeping room for his own happiness. He gambled big and he found something he never dreamed of for himself.

John was working on a job he didn't like. Yet, he didn't really have time to find one that he wanted. He didn't even know for sure what he'd like to do. He had been an insurance salesman for most of his working life. He began shortly after he got out of the army.

"Sometimes I'd like to tell the boss to get lost. The pressures to produce are more than any normal person can take," he explained.

John wasn't a quitter, but he had sense enough to realize that there was something very wrong about his situation. "Let's try a long shot," I suggested to him. He was so full of frustration and hatred for his job that he couldn't think clearly about what kind of work he would like. He didn't know what he'd prefer. He was in the grips of a vicious circle and he knew it.

"Can you afford to hand in your resignation and *then* look for something else?" I asked him. "I'll teach you how to activate Cosmosis for yourself."

"I can exist for a month or two on what I've saved, and my wife is working part-time," he said.

He took the plunge. John handed in his resignation. It took a lot of courage to do that. He had no other job in mind, no offers for a job, no idea of what he was better suited for. To be frank about it, he was putting himself in a corner. But, he was also *making room* for his new desire to take shape in his consciousness.

For the first week of his unemployment, he did absolutely nothing, except work on the simple exercise of Cosmosis.

John rested, slept late, probably ate too much, and got to know himself. His wife, who graciously supported his move to find new work in this unorthodox way, found to her surprise that she was married to a new person.

He was relaxed, happy, and he displayed an up-beat personality and a brand-new optimism. The second week he started to look for work.

Within three weeks after John started his job search, he found just what he wanted. He landed a job as a newspaper space salesman.

Within a year's time, his income had doubled with the extra commissions that he earned! It suited him to a "T." What had he done? He had forced out failure and made room for success. It was a big chance, but he gambled and won not only peace of mind and happiness but greater financial independence as well. It couldn't have worked out better.

So, our first step in making everything you do become

positive is: *Make space for positive experience by getting rid of what you do not like in your life.*

A PROGRAM TO GIVE YOU MORE ROOM
FOR POSITIVE ACTION

Step 1

Here is a checklist for a program to help you make sure you have all the mental and emotional space for those positive experiences that Cosmosis can attract for you:

1. Remove time spent on fruitless projects and activities.
2. Remove thoughts which limit your creativity or your options.
3. Remove contacts with people who are failures.

Once you've cleared the air and given yourself some elbowroom, you are ready to influence future events to bring your desire into being. You are ready to think about your goals, the steps you'll take to realize your desire.

1. Give yourself time to think, to ponder, to drift.
2. Give yourself some activities which are different, unlike those in which you usually engage.
3. Meet some new people or contact someone you haven't seen in a long time.
4. Before you use the freed space, time, or energy, wait to see what develops.

Step 2

The second step in making everything you do become positive is: *Increase your awareness of just what is positive*

70

and what is negative. Go back over the last five years of your life and ask yourself these two questions:

1. *What experiences, people, and opportunities multiplied themselves into satisfying and rewarding conditions for my growth and development as a person?*

2. *What experiences, people, and opportunities multiplied themselves into disharmonious and unrewarding conditions for me?*

Anything which harms your image of yourself is something to be avoided. On the other hand, any experience which increases your self-esteem, or makes you feel better about yourself, is a positive experience and should be repeated.

Sometimes our sense of competition directs us to goals which are impossible to reach. But, when we do the natural thing, that which is easy for us, we are pleased with the result. Our self-evaluation is good! But challenges which are impossible for us to accept simply create a failure complex in our thinking, and our self-image goes down. Forget your failures and don't let yourself get into negative circumstances in the future.

Step 3

The third step in making everything you do become positive is: *Be sure to set goals which are positive.*

"But wait a minute," you may be saying to yourself. "How will you use both positive and negative circumstances if you set only positive goals? Where does knowledge of the negative fit in?"

Goals should be positive. But negation can be used in *negative circumstances* to help you get into a positive frame of mind. In other words, you can fight fire with fire. Let's look at a case history that explains this idea.

71

HOW TO USE NEGATION
AS A PROTECTIVE DEVICE

Negation is a defensive tactic. Let's assume you selected positive goals, goals which allow you to express your own unique qualities and increase your self-esteem. How would you use negation as a practical strategy in everyday living?

**How Judy Used Negation
in Her Program**

Judy's was a classic case which is seen in homes around the world.

Judy was a newly married girl in her early twenties. She and her husband were just settling down in a small suburban home. They'd been in the home about six months. Everything was running smoothly, on the surface at least.

But there was interference developing from an outside source. It was coming from a "nosey" neighbor who just wanted to advise and help.

The neighbor—we shall call her Alice—carried stories of gloom and doom. She was the local gossip columnist. I'm sure you know the type. But, that wasn't the worst part of the situation. Alice was slowly moving Judy's thinking into a negative channel.

For example, Judy would be chock full of enthusiasm about something—her vacation next year, or an appliance she'd planned to purchase, or a party she and her husband were going to attend.

But, each time Judy talked about her plans, there was Alice, asking a dozen questions, pointing out pitfalls, exaggerating the hazards and dangers.

The more Judy tried to justify her decisions or intentions, the more Alice would jump on her plans and raise doubts and imaginary frustrations.

Finally, Judy hit on a "fight fire with fire" philosophy. It created a dramatic change in her relationship with Alice and it protected Judy from further negation.

Here is what she did, upon my advice—and I'm sure she did it with a secret twinkle in her eye. Each time Alice inserted a doubt or negative statement in the conversation, Judy simply *turned the idea around and asked Alice the same question about something she was planning to do.*

Here are some typical ways that this tactic worked for Judy.

Alice would say that Judy's vacation was planned at the wrong time of the year. Judy would ask when Alice was planning hers and point out how it was wrong.

Alice would maintain that a certain appliance Judy had in mind was the wrong brand, or the wrong model for her needs. Judy would ask what brand Alice had and raise numerous questions about its usefulness.

This technique worked so well for Judy that she wasn't pestered with these picky, petty conversations anymore. Alice simply went to someone else to sell her negative thinking.

This case points up the tremendous power of negative thinking. And it shows that *there are times when only the effective reversal of the negation will protect you.* When you reverse a negation, you are fighting fire with fire. You are using the tactics of the enemy in order to beat him at his own game.

POINTS TO REMEMBER FROM THIS CHAPTER

1. The fundamental source of universal power can manifest itself in either positive or negative forms.

73

2. A personal inventory tells you where you are and where you'd like to be so you can begin realizing your inner desires.

3. The first step in making everything you do become positive is to get rid of what you don't like to make room for your desires.

4. The second step is to be aware of what is positive and what is negative, judged by your past experience.

5. The third step is to set goals which are positive.

6. Negation can be used as a protective device against negative thinkers.

Chapter 5

HOW TO DEVELOP
OCCULT POWER WITH COSMOSIS

Would you like to possess power beyond the bounds of ordinary knowledge? Power disclosed not by inspection but by experimentation? Power that puts you in a class all by yourself? The power of the universe, of nature, that astounds, amazes, and delights? Power that is fantastic to others but ordinary to you?

This chapter is about the unusual, the mysterious, the aspects of Cosmosis that you, and you alone, can experience by taking the usual Cosmosis theory to its logical conclusion—mastery of Cosmosis.

Here is the secret doctrine of Cosmosis, the laws which can put you in the same league with great thinkers throughout history.

Occult power is different from other forms of psychic power in that *it is a power of continuous revelation.* It is revealed every second of every day to the one who is the master. *It is living in a state of eternal receptivity to Cosmosis.*

What is the starting point for the revelation of occult knowledge?

The starting point is a *power base*—a group of people devoted to the secret revelations of Cosmosis, the revelations which cannot be given to the general public for fear that they may be misused.

This chapter will show you how to form such a group, what to do, and how to develop these powers which stagger the imagination.

From a Cosmic point of view, a chain is as strong as its weakest link. A group of friends working together can amass power which is ten times as great as the power you can generate on your own. However, you may proceed on your own if you wish.

EXAMPLES OF OCCULT POWER
GENERATED BY GROUPS

One occult study group was able to achieve, in a year's time, the following psychic achievements for its seven members:

1. The total yearly income of the members increased by 35%.
2. Two members became married and they are very happy.
3. Five significant healings occurred—two of which were verified by medical doctors.
4. Out-of-body experiences by one member of the group enabled one person to be a channel for the higher forces. These forces took over the leadership of the group to teach the secrets which led to many new demonstrations of occult power.
5. The most success was with the regulation of thought-forms of those outside the group. The study group was able to influence the actions and attitudes of people

outside the group who were unaware of this hidden influence.

We will examine the details of these examples later in this chapter. But, first, let's see what steps you can take to get started.

STEPS TO TAKE TO START
AN OCCULT STUDY GROUP

A group can begin occult work with only three people. Seven is an excellent number but some groups get to be as high as 13.

Decide on a specific time each week that you can meet quietly and secretly. An evening hour during the middle of the week is ideal. At the first meeting, dedicate yourselves to helping each other. Open yourselves in meditation to guidance from the higher levels and swear absolute trust in these higher intelligences. Outsiders should never know what you are doing—or why. When you have success, keep it to yourselves or you will find your power draining out and not renewing itself.

A GENERAL OUTLINE FOR YOUR
OCCULT GROUP MEETING

1. Play quiet background music as the members of the group assemble. Try not to discuss anything which pertains to the work until you are actually conducting the meeting.
2. Light a candle, or candles, stand, join hands, and pray that you will be led into the "way of truth" to help each other and to be instruments for the highest Cosmic forces.
3. Be seated, extinguish your candles, and conduct the remainder of the meeting in darkness.
4. Practice the Kundalini exercises mentioned in Chapter 1.

5. Sit in silence until a member of the group is led to speak with the impressions, ideas, or feelings which come to mind. All material—no matter how insignificant—should be shared verbally with the other members of the group. Slowly, a basic message or pattern will emerge which becomes the spiritual guidance which the group is seeking. As the members grow in awareness of the Cosmic forces, more material will be forthcoming and each member will be a channel for the message work.

6. When it comes time to conclude, stand and pray that you will be kept safely until the next meeting.

7. Frequently the group will be directed to do something, such as recite certain incantations or perform rituals for the demonstration of further occult power.

HOW TO USE INCANTATIONS, RITUALS, AND SPIRIT MESSENGERS

Incantations are chants which have power. *A ritual* is the repetition of a set form in a religious or mystical rite. *Spiritual messengers* are the agents of the higher Cosmic forces who carry out the work which they are called upon to do by incantation and ritual.

A ritual or incantation is of greater power if it is used in the name of an established Cosmic power. For example, an incantation addressed to a lesser figure does not evoke as much concentrated power as one addressed to a well-established luminary.

Rituals, which are performed in the likeness of established rituals, bear the vibrational imprint of the similarity. Early Christians utilized the Jewish Sedar Service, or Passover Feast, in the development of the Last Supper or Holy Communion.

Likewise, there are rituals within all religions which have been used since the beginning of mankind. Universal themes occur in incantations as well.

Our purpose here is to extract these universal elements

and reformulate them for your own personal use.

All religions have as their object contact with the Supreme Being, or God. We refer to this quest as a desire to establish harmony between man and the universe.

Cosmosis is the energy of Ultimate Reality or the Spirit of God; therefore, these universal rituals and incantations which can be used by your group *do not conflict with any religion.* In fact, they are the very elements which almost all religions have in common, because they are valid as they stand. They help establish a relationship between man and the Cosmos, or God.

A RITUAL FOR INCREASED PROSPERITY

1. Prepare a table to be used as an altar.
2. Light a candle and call on the Cosmosis-inspired spirit messengers to assist you in the creation of prosperity.
3. Burn a dollar bill, a check, or some other symbol of prosperity as a sacrifice. As the flame dies out, repeat the name of the person for whom this ritual was performed. Dispose of the ashes by placing them in the ground. Repeat this ritual once every 13 days until prosperity comes into the life of the person for whom the ritual was requested.

A RITUAL FOR GREATER LOVE
BETWEEN THE SEXES

1. Prepare a table to be used as an altar.
2. Light a candle and call on the Cosmosis-inspired spirit messengers to assist you in bringing about greater love (name the people).
3. Burn a small part of a garment worn by each person. As the flame dies out, repeat the names of the two people three times. Dispose of the ashes by placing them in the

79

ground. Repeat this ritual once every 13 days until greater love has been expressed between the persons for whom the ritual was performed.

A RITUAL FOR BETTER HEALTH

1. Prepare a table to be used as an altar.
2. Light a candle and call on the Cosmosis-inspired spirit messengers to assist you in bringing about better health (name the person).
3. Burn anything which is symbolic of the ailment. Dispose of the ashes by placing them in the ground. Repeat this ritual once every 13 days until better health has been realized.

A RITUAL FOR PEACE OF MIND
AND BETTER HUMAN RELATIONS

1. Prepare a table to be used as an altar.
2. Light a candle and call on the Cosmosis-inspired spirit messengers to assist you in bringing about peace of mind and better human relations (name the person).
3. Burn a small paper with the person's signature on it. Or you may burn a small photograph of the person. Dispose of the ashes as described above. Repeat the ritual as often as necessary.

A RITUAL FOR REVERSING
A NEGATIVE CONDITION

1. Prepare a table as described in previous rituals.
2. Light a candle and call on the spirit messengers as above.
3. Burn something which is symbolic of the negative condition and proceed in the same manner described in the previous rituals. Repeat this ritual once every 13 days until the negative condition has been removed.

How Gordon Used These Rituals
to Gain Everything

Gordon was a man in his early thirties, married, and the father of two children. He worked in a steel mill in a good hourly job. His family resided in a modest home in the suburbs of a large city.

Gordon needed several things to make his life complete. He needed more money to keep his family secure and to provide for the future education of his children. He was troubled with a tired feeling, too. Gordon wanted more pep, better health, and stamina to carry on with a rigorous work schedule.

A meaningful spiritual life was one of Gordon's goals; he longed for the peace of mind of having found God's expression in his own life.

He used the rituals in our group for prosperity, health, and peace of mind. He knew Cosmosis could work directly for him and he called on the Cosmosis-infused higher intelligences to assist in supercharging his life with the transformation of Cosmosis, the eternal life energy of the universe.

The spirit messengers didn't let him down.

He was so thankful for what happened—all in a short time—that he couldn't stop talking about it. His entire being radiated with joy and new confidence in himself and his future.

First he got a promotion to a management position. He made contact with a spirit entity that gave him new health and energy and a feeling of protection and peace of mind. The entity that appeared to him as he performed the ritual seemed to be a master from the Far East. The spirit gave the name Rama and appeared to Gordon's inner vision or mind's eye, to give him special guidance, words of advice, and healing vitality.

81

How the Rituals Failed
to Work for Laura

Faith in Cosmosis, the spirit messengers, and in these rituals inevitably leads to success. But, failure to take these simple methods seriously can lead to failure and even to reversal into a negative cycle. Such was the case with Laura, a beautiful woman in her early forties, divorced, and living with her married daughter.

Laura worked as a public stenographer and was able to contribute financially to the household. She kept to herself and didn't meddle in the affairs of her daughter's marriage. She had her own group of friends and they took vacations, went to the theater, and attended other social affairs together.

The circumstances of Laura's undoing were simple. She met an attorney who had his offices in her building. They met accidentally while they were having lunch.

Time passed and they began to see more and more of each other.

The only hitch in their closeness and the fondness which was developing was that the attorney was married. Complications set in. Laura fell deeply in love with the man. He felt love for her but he *also* was in love with his own wife.

Laura heard about the rituals from a friend of hers who was in one of our development groups. She asked her friend to help create more love between them. But, she was not honest in her request—*she did not explain that the attorney was already married.*

In Laura's case the rituals backfired. If she had full faith in them, she never would have hidden the facts from her friend who was in the group. Instead she adopted an attitude of "every little bit helps." She did not place full faith in the rituals or she would have disclosed all of the facts so that the metaphysical work would have been supportive instead of negative.

The spirit messengers of Cosmosis retalifited by causing the attorney to go back to his wife, leaving Laura alone and brokenhearted. She admitted afterward that she asked the group to do the work just to "see what would happen."

A WARNING ABOUT THE ILL EFFECTS OF TOO MUCH POWER

As we pointed out earlier, a group can tap into more Cosmic energy than an individual. Calling on the spiritual messengers in the higher realms doesn't simply put your desire into their hands. There is judgement involved also. They will work out the best circumstances for all concerned. They do not simply "rubber stamp" everything that the group suggests. If you try to hide something from them or use their power to damage someone or destroy something loving, creative, or good, you may find the worst kind of retribution from their action. Make sure your motives are pure and your intentions positive before you undertake to perform these rituals.

HOW TO REGULATE THOUGHT-FORMS WITH COSMOSIS

Did you know that nothing you do is free from the influence of your subconscious mind?

It was the great psychoanalyst, Sigmund Freud, who discovered that we are all under the domination of the "hidden" part of our minds.

Your subconscious—when properly directed and controlled through Cosmosis energizing—is one of your greatest assets in getting the things you want from life now.

83

Your subconscious can help you get rid of unwanted habits; it can help you improve your efficiency, make you a more appealing personality, and assist you in attracting success.

Your subconscious mind can be directed to help you do the following things when it is boosted with Cosmosis:

* Create a sparkling personality.
* Gain or lose weight.
* Stop smoking.
* Bring out hidden talents.
* Overcome a detrimental habit.
* Increase your "sales-ability" to make more money.
* Make your love life "click" for total satisfaction.

Your subconscious is using Cosmosis "imprints"— your heritage as a human—to:

* Keep you breathing, your heart beating, and your metabolism working properly to send nourishment throughout your body.
* Regulate your digestion of food, your blood pressure, the reflex muscles of your body, and your sympathetic nervous system.
* Repair worn-out tissues and keep the body organs working in balance with each other.

THE REAL SECRET WEAPON
IN YOUR SUBCONSCIOUS

Your subconscious mind has a potent secret weapon which it can put to work for you right away if you know the Cosmic key.

The secret weapon of your subconscious mind is the fact that it takes orders from your conscious mind without

84

question. Your subconscious mind will carry out your orders automatically without any question.

Your conscious mind is your reasoning mind, your doubting mind, the "second guessing" mind. But your subconscious mind accepts any visualized thought-form which you give it and it *acts on that thought-form.*

Since your thought-forms do reach out and influence other people and situations near you, it is possible to double and triple your occult power by regulating the thought-forms being broadcast from your subconscious mind.

HOW TO REACH AND CONTROL
YOUR SUBCONSCIOUS THOUGHT-FORMS

You are controlling your subconscious thought-forms at this very moment.

Your most often repeated thoughts formed in the conscious mind are setting up a reflection in the subconscious. Everything you say or do, read, write, or think leaves a trace in the subconscious.

Self-suggestion and deep concentration will influence your subconscious.

Repetition is the key technique to use in summoning the power of your subconscious to control your thought-forms.

Write a thought down and read it over and over. Concentrate on a thought while you are alone and quiet.

Saying positive thoughts out loud increases the self-suggestive influence you will exercise over your thought-forms.

Here are some tips and hints on reaching your subconscious through self-suggestion and repetition.

1. *Repel any negative thoughts that you have* or that anyone close to you tries to force on you.
2. *Try not to react to people with hatred, suspicion, or*

mistrust. These emotional reactions often start a chain reaction of negation power which can bring into your life the very things you are trying to avoid.

3. *Emphasize your own success* and your own ability to handle life's problems. You can overcome difficulties and you can bring the *right* kind of life into being.

4. *Allow only positive information into your life.* Avoid violent and disturbing news, books that deal with crime and twisted personalities, and people who talk constantly about life's threatening side.

5. *Start a self-improvement program* of reading, attending lectures, and implanting beneficial thoughts. Keep yourself inspired and working toward a better life by being informed on the latest self-improvement literature and material. Parker Publishing Company, Inc., the publisher of this book, is one of the world's largest suppliers of excellent material in this field.

How Harriet Saved Her Family with Subconscious Cosmosis Control

Harriet V. saved her family from alienation and disaster by using subconscious thought-form control. She was married to a successful corporate attorney in a fashionable suburb. Her three teen-age sons were living at home and going to high school. They were restive because of the discipline of their father and his lack of understanding of their needs as growing individuals.

The lack of communication between the father and his sons was so great, that day after day might pass without any more conversations between them than necessity demanded.

The oldest boy wanted a car of his own which he could afford by spending his summer earnings. His father objected. The boy's desire for a car became a focal point for dissent by the two younger sons. They were all in total agreement concerning the father's objection which they felt was unreasonable.

Harriet was in the middle of the disagreement. She influenced her own subconscious thought-forms so that she could be *calm* during this stormy period. She hoped to be able to suggest a *solution* to help overcome the impasse.

She wrote down the following message to herself: "I will remain calm during all discussions between myself and members of my family. A positive solution will be found that will bring my husband and our sons back together again." She carried this message with her at all times and she read it to herself at least once each hour during the day. Sometimes she read it over and over out loud. Harriet knew the laws of Cosmosis, and she had faith in the power of her subconscious mind to release the thought-form so it could be reflected in family discussions.

Her husband made the decision that broke the ice.

He said to Harriet, "We can't let this animosity and mistrust build any longer. Why don't we all sit down and talk this through? We've got to reach some agreement. It is ridiculous for us to live like this."

Harriet talked to the boys and set a time for a family conference.

They all got together at the dining room table and discussed their differences. Within minutes Harriet was moderating the dispute and trying to reach an understanding of each person's needs and desires.

She helped convince her husband to let the oldest boy have a car. Harmony was established and communication became open. Each member of the family, the boys and their father included, vowed to try to understand the other's point of view.

Harriet's family meets for a "conference" like this each week. Many differences get ironed out before they have a chance to get out of proportion. There is an open quality and a relaxed atmosphere about these meetings. Relationships are less strained and much more trust exists between the boys and their parents.

HOW TO CREATE
OUT-OF-BODY EXPERIENCES

Astral projection or out-of-body experiences will take you to distant places so that you can see and hear just as if you were physically present.

Cosmosis energy causes these astral traveling experiences by apparently detaching the astral body, or etheric double, from the physical body and moving to a different time-space location.

Astral projection can be used to:

* Travel at will to locations of friends and participate in their activities.
* Travel to foreign lands and distant places to see what is happening and influence those present with your desires.
* Change your location in time, as well as move backward to an historical moment to experience it as if you were there.
* Go forward in time to see new civilizations, other planets, and maintain contact with superior intelligences.
* Converse with a great personality, a leader, teacher, artist, or musician who has passed into the Higher Realms.

THE MASTER TECHNIQUE
FOR ASTRAL PROJECTION

Here is the technique for astral projection. This master key lets Cosmosis energy do all the work. You are safely transported to other locations in time and space and returned to your earthly body by Cosmic energy. You do not have to navigate the trip or worry about what is happening to you. This technique is safe *as long as you are in good health and have a stable mental attitude.* If you are under a doctor's care, have a history of mental disorder, or a chronic physical complaint, do not use this method.

Following are the five steps to take:

1. *Select a Time or Place That You Would Like to Visit.* You may find nearby locations easier to make contact with than foreign locations. People and places that you are familiar with have an emotional and associative "charge" about them which makes them easier to attune with.

2. *Fix Firmly in Your Conscious Mind a Positive Attitude with Respect to the Place You Have Selected.* Do this even before you are ready to create the projection. Then ask several friends to help you by being present as Cosmic batteries the first few times you try projecting your etheric double.

3. *Now You Are Ready to Take Your First Trip.* Late evening is the ideal time to project. Lie flat on a couch with a single candle on a table so that you can comfortably gaze into its rays. Ask your friends to sit near you but not close enough to distract you.

4. *Stare into the Candle and Let Your Entire Being Fall into the Light of the Flame.* Relax and breathe deeply as you feel a heavy sensation coming over you. You will go into a light state of trance. As you feel yourself becoming more and more sleepy, direct your mind's attention on the destination.

5. *You Will Feel Your Etheric Body Detach and Then You Will Be in a Dream World Where You Will See What Is Happening in Your New Time-Space Location.* When you have concluded your observation and influence at the destination, you will automatically be brought back to your physical body by the power of Cosmosis. You do

not need to worry about coming "out" of the trance, either. When your trip has been concluded you will awake refreshed, with your etheric body hovering around your physical body.

Astral Projection Case Histories That Prove the Benefits

Mrs. W.Z. used the astral projection master technique to influence her husband while he was undergoing heart surgery. She helped calm and reassure her husband as well as give the doctors and nurses additional psychic support. The operation was a success and Mr. Z. is alive and well today. He claims that he knew his wife was with him during the critical surgery.

Mr. T.R. used astral travel to visit Egyptian pyramids and to look inside to gain their secrets. Today, he channels the information about the ancient wisdom of the Egyptians from manuscripts he "reads" while he is visiting the tombs. He travels most often while he is sleeping. But, he can also do it at will.

Bob Q. maintains daily contact with supreme intelligences from outer space who are interplanetary travelers. He knows and understands their mission and is now trying to make direct contact with the beings who are piloting the flying saucers that are observing earth. Much of his information is secret of course, but he keeps elaborate records and tape recordings of actual conversations he holds while on these trips. A personality by the name of Skarta beams in on him and assists in taking him to various planes of existence.

Astral projection can be one of the most satisfying and meaningful psychic powers. Cosmosis can give it to you. But, bear in mind that this power is an advanced one that not everyone is able to demonstrate. It requires diligent practice. The rewards are fantastic in the areas of gaining higher wisdom and knowledge, which is revealed during these soul flights. Continuous revelation comes to the occult practitioner who is able to master this most fascinating power of all—the power of astral travel.

POINTS TO REMEMBER FROM THIS CHAPTER

1. Occult power is complete mastery of Cosmosis. In order to have this power, a group of people must meet to pool their energies and efforts.

2. An occult study group uses incantations, rituals, and spirit messengers to bring prosperity, love, health, and better human relations into being. Negative conditions can also be reversed.

3. Thoughts can be controlled through the subconscious use of Cosmosis. You can control your thoughts as well as other people's.

4. Out-of-body experiences enable you to go anywhere in time or space and act as a participant in events to influence them in your favor.

5. Astral travel also gives you access to higher wisdom and knowledge.

Chapter 6

HOW COSMOSIS ATTRACTS PROSPERITY AND BUSINESS SUCCESS

Money isn't everything, but life is easier when you have enough of it!

This chapter will show you how to apply the laws of Cosmosis to make money, keep money, and multiply it. By using the suggestions in this chapter, you can be the richest person you know.

Prosperity is easy to achieve. Much easier than most people think. It can be easy for you, no matter what your condition in life. Before you start to evidence prosperity there is one all-important, major step to take. Without this step in your consciousness, you cannot attract money—no matter how hard you try. The wealthiest people in the world have taken this step in their thinking. It will help you apply the laws in this chapter if you can make this step *now*.

THE FIRST STEP IN ATTRACTING, HOLDING, AND MULTIPLYING MONEY

The first step to take is *get rid of your guilt about being*

93

rich! It is not "out of divine order" for you to be wealthy. You are entitled to be rich, just as rich as the next person. In fact, you can be richer now, if you can take this first step. There is nothing wrong about having money. Being poor or in financial distress is not necessarily good. *It is wrong not to have enough money.* It is *right* to have money, and lots of it!

HOW TO FEEL GOOD
ABOUT HAVING MONEY

1. *Think About the Things Money Can Do for Yourself and Others.* All of the world's most wealthy people used money to do something other than satisfy their own needs. Rockefeller, Ford, Carnegie, and Mellon all used their money to accomplish a greater good for many people, for all of humanity in many cases. Money cannot be the driving force in your life, but it can motivate your drive.

2. *List All the Things You Want Which Money Can Get for You.* Keep this list handy and refer to it each day. When you change from one activity to another, remind yourself that "time is money" and that "time spent gaining money is good."

3. *Study the Lives of Wealthy Men.* You'll see that they are just as human as you are. They had strengths and weaknesses, failures and successes. As a starter try reading the biographies of Vanderbilt, Astor, Gould, Getty, Hearst, Morgenthau, Baruch, and Edison.

WHY SOME PEOPLE ARE WEALTHY
AND OTHERS ARE POOR

Money is a medium of exchange. As such it is an expression of a need and the ability to meet that need. Let's say you need a loaf of bread. Your need is expressed in the form of the price of that bread. The seller's price to you is his expression of his ability to meet that need.

From a Cosmic viewpoint there is always enough money to meet any need, since the ability to meet that need is infinite and never ending. Simply stated, there is actually no limit on the amount of money. Obtaining that unlimited supply for your needs is the problem.

Wealthy people have found the need which must be met, then they meet that need and obtain money for it. They are able to think creatively, so they locate new needs and new ways that these needs can be met.

A person becomes poor when he cannot think about others' needs and the actions that can be taken *by him* to help meet those needs.

THE LAW OF MONEY CONSCIOUSNESS

Wealth is attracted and accumulated by means of a Cosmic law called "Money Consciousness." Money is in the hands of those who are aware, consciously or unconsciously, of this mental state of Money Consciousness.

The Law of Money Consciousness is expressed by this formula:

YOUR ABILITY TO MEET THE NEED +
DEMAND FOR THE NEED =
YOUR ABILITY TO MAKE MONEY.

There are many things you could do right now to make money. But, *one* thing you could do would make *more* money than anything else because the demand for *that* service is *greatest*.

Money also attracts money. The more money you have, the more you are likely to get. Why? Because your options are greater. Even your power to borrow money is greater if you have money.

A woman I know who is a widow spends much of her time worrying about money and how she will make ends meet. Consequently, she is fearful of losing money and spends only the barest minimum on the essentials. One of the things she has skimped on has been her own food. Today she is in the hospital with malnutrition. The cost of her stay is impossible to calculate. If she had spent, freely, a few dollars a week to maintain her diet and health, she might not be losing thousands for medical treatment. She had developed an incorrect Money Consciousness. She was "fixated" on the idea of savings in order to "hold on" to things.

The right kind of "Money Consciousness"—the kind that helps money to multiply—is the kind that will take risks, moderate risks. A student of metaphysics who is in one of our study groups invested several thousand dollars in some acreage near an inland lake. He sold the property at double the price he paid when the area opened up to those looking for a place to build summer homes. He took this risk because he had *faith* that the money would be returned—in *multiplied* form, one way or another.

Faith

HOW TO DEVELOP A WEALTH-PRODUCING MONEY CONSCIOUSNESS

1. *Don't Be Afraid of Money.* Don't be afraid to spend money constructively in line with your program to become wealthier.
2. *Keep Yourself Financially Informed.* Read the business sections of magazines and newspapers. Even the classified ads in daily papers can yield stimulating financial ideas. One idea may be enough to spark an entire series of creative surges that concludes with more cash in your bank account.

96

③ *Associate with People Who Have More Money Than You Do.* Don't do this to keep up with these people. You cannot "outspend" people who are wealthier than you are. You *can* see how they are managing their money, how they are alert to opportunities, and how they are increasing their financial positions. Success breeds success, and just the mere association with those on a higher financial plateau will automatically aid and stimulate your Money Consciousness.

④ *Look for Bargains.* Never spend money just to satisfy your own ego requirements. Try not to buy things when you are in a low period or when you feel "down in the dumps." Panic buying may put you further behind the eightball. Do look for bargains; compare before you buy. Shop for major and small purchases with this motto in mind—"compare prices, compare values, compare your long-term commitment." Remember that advertising which entices you to *save* is actually encouraging you to *spend.*

⑤ *Save and Reinvest Your Money. Don't just save your money.* Put it to use earning more money for you. If you have extra money, more than you need, resist the temptation to buy something big. Also, be careful of investment schemes that promise you that you can make a killing. Consult a professional investment counselor before you go into anything that seems suspicious. There are many people ready and willing to take everything you have on promises alone. Wise saving and wise investment will put you into a financial position that will pay handsome dividends.

HOW COSMOSIS MAKES YOU FREE
TO SPECULATE AND TAKE RISKS

There are many ways that Cosmosis can help you improve your financial position. One way is to let it work for you in giving you the elbowroom financially to take risks and speculate.

Following is the technique for speculation with the help of Cosmosis:

1. *Sit Quietly in Meditation.* Be sure you'll not be interrupted by anything. Breathe deeply and evenly. Focus the Cosmic energy at the base of the spine by visualizing it gathering there.

2. *Let the Kundalini Energy Move up the Spine Until It Radiates Around the Head.* You have had instructions on this in an earlier chapter.

3. *When You Are Able to See, in Your Mind's Eye, the Kundalini Running Through Your Brain, Pray and Affirm with Confidence That You Will Be Led into the Right Speculative Decision.* Be sure to write down your impressions as you receive them. This is an important procedure—and save these written impressions for future reference in shaping your wealth program.

This technique has worked wonders for others. But it cannot be used as a last resort. Be sure you are in a strong financial position so that you can afford to speculate with your money. If you cannot afford to lose, don't speculate. Chances are most in your favor if you are not down to your last few dollars. Any speculation done in haste is often wasted.

How Halena Won $500 at a Raffle

Halena X. was a high school language teacher who had a few extra dollars to speculate with. She performed the Cosmosis method outlined here. She simply prayed and affirmed that she might be led to invest her money in a wise security on the New York Stock Exchange. She had the money to lose and she wanted to speculate with it in order to cash in on this Cosmosis technique.

Halena's case showed how mysterious Cosmosis can

be. She received the psychic impression that she should go to her local church's bingo game and raffle. The bingo game and raffle were being held the next evening as a benefit for charity. The top prize was $500.

She went to the church, bought a ticket, and started to play bingo. Later in the evening a raffle was held. All the tickets sold were placed in a large container and drawn out one by one for the top prizes. Everyone was expectant and a hush fell over the crowd.

The very first number called for the top prize of $500 was Halena's.

She didn't win anything at Bingo.

Her total expenditure for the evening was about $6. But she gained $494 dollars in one evening.

It was a small speculation that paid off *big* under the guidance of Cosmosis forces!

How Ken Speculated with Land
That Paid Off Handsomely

Ken T., an attorney, was guided to purchase some suburban land with trees and a stream running through the property. He hoped to sell it to a developer for a housing subdivision.

The simple Cosmosis exercise did the trick for him.

Cosmosis gave him a triple surprise, though, when he learned that a gas company wanted to buy the mineral rights and tap a large natural gas reserve under the property.

Ken sold the property itself and made a 300 per cent profit on it.

How One Speculation Turned
into a Big Loss

Cosmosis doesn't always work just the way we want it

to as these cases point out. If we deliberately misuse it, we may be in a worse state than if we hadn't called on the Cosmic force at all.

Here is an example of disregarding the psychic impressions that came from Cosmosis and as a result failing to speculate profitably.

Mrs. S.G. invoked Cosmosis to improve her speculative position. Her mistake arose from the fact that she had a special investment in mind *before* she asked for Cosmosis help. She was fixated on a certain industrial stock investment.

She followed the Cosmosis steps outlined earlier without any deviation. But for some unexplained reason she didn't get any impression at all. She felt the Kundalini rising to her brain and she asked the great powers that she be led to big profits. Her problem was that the Cosmosis forces were trying to tell her to do nothing at all by not giving her any impressions. She mistook this lack of specific direction as a sign that she was to go ahead with her investment plan. She took her money and purchased the stock she had in mind, only to find that within six months' time it dwindled in value to less than one-third the price she paid for it.

The lesson she learned quite graciously from this adverse experience was that often if a Cosmosis exercise or directive doesn't work exactly as expected, there is a very significant reason—in this case Mrs. S.G. was being told to wait.

Most psychic powers are that way. As miraculous as they are and as valuable as Cosmic forces can be, there is a law of balance and equilibrium at work. One must be in accord with that law in order to be a real instrument for Cosmosis. If your motives are true and your intentions are pure you will advance in Cosmic understanding, just as the great thinkers of all time have done. You can start with what you have, where you are, to use this masterful power—*as long as you can devote yourself physically, emotionally, spiritually, and intellectually to the dictates of Cosmosis.* The Living Infinite will be your partner if you give It half a chance to work with you. You cannot always dictate to It. It knows what is best for you. Have faith in It and all will work out well.

HOW TO PUT THE COSMOSIS FORTUNE MULTIPLIER TECHNIQUE TO WORK

All the radiant splendor of true wealth can be yours by applying the Cosmosis Fortune Multiplier technique. This psychic secret, carefully revealed only to initiated students in ancient lands and esoteric cultures, is revealed here for you for perhaps the first time in your life.

This wisdom has been hidden from the masses of people, and its secrets have been jealously guarded and withheld.

As a general basis, civilization depends on the accumulation and use of wealth in its various forms.

But you can exist without accumulated wealth. As an individual, you can exist without a great deal of money and still survive. This is the clue to the Cosmosis Fortune Multiplier technique. Great sages and mental and spiritual giants knew this fact—and most of them had enough money, sometimes much more than they needed.

You, too, can exist without dependence on money. When you actually depend on money you are a victim to the methods you must use to get it.

That is the secret. When you *ignore* money for money's sake alone, you will automatically place emphasis on something far more important—you, your growth and development as a person in the Cosmosis concept.

In other words, place your emphasis on the things that count. When you make wealth your master, you are a slave to it.

The Cosmosis Fortune Multiplier technique is this: Use money—*but do not depend on it!*

If financial matters have a hold over you at this moment, then your future happiness is at stake. You are in trouble if money has become the only major drive in your life.

You may know of people who plan and scheme for an entire lifetime to gain money only to be too old or ill to enjoy it.

Those that have a fortune are those that have true happiness. If you are happy, money will multiply itself for you.

The great Cosmic guardians can take care of you for the rest of your life if you will call on them with Cosmosis. Once you've turned your fortune over to these higher intelligences, it will multiply.

Important!

THE SECRET OF THE AGES— HOW TO USE MONEY WITHOUT DEPENDING ON IT

Here is how you can multiply your fortune by using money without depending on it. These tips will save you money and increase your financial standing.

1. *Set aside* a small amount of money to use as *seed money*. Plant this seed money on a regular basis with some charity or religious institution. Or, simply use it to help someone. Try giving it away freely to be of service to your fellowman. Remember, money too, as any article, has a soul.

2. *Don't* use all the *credit* that you've got. It is easy to buy things on credit—from the family car, to your house, home furnishings, and even your vacation—all can be enjoyed before you can afford them. No matter what your annual income, the temptation to overspend is there. Resist the temptation and stick to the essentials.

102

3. If you need something, *pray* that your need will be met. Don't pray directly for money but *do ask for what you need* through prayer. God does supply all wants and needs. But the great Infinite Intelligence which is in all things needs to know by *your* request what should be made manifest. The Bible puts it well by saying, "Seek and you shall find. Knock and it shall be opened to you."

ONE OF THE POOREST PERSONS I KNOW

One of the poorest persons I know is a Mexican woman who reads palms in a poverty section of a large city. Her only income is from donations which her friends give her for her advice and encouragement. Warm and outgoing, her ethical conduct is beyond reproach. She uses money to help others as well as herself. It is only a means to an end, not an end in itself. She considers herself wealthy because all of her needs are met as soon as they arise. She does not depend on money to solve her problems. It is there and she uses it.

ONE OF THE WEALTHIEST
PERSONS I KNOW

One of the wealthiest persons I know does the same thing. He is retired from a corporate officer's job but is quite active in civic affairs. His private life consists of trying to decide how to give some of his large fortune away. As he puts it, "I have everything I need. But the world needs to be improved. I am doing my part by using my resources, money, to improve the lot of mankind." He is using money, but he is not dependent upon it himself.

You may not be the poorest person in your community, nor the wealthiest, but you can view every financial decision in the same way. Ask yourself this question: *Is the action I'm taking going to make me dependent on money or will it make me free to use it?*

ENERGIZING YOUR LIFE
WITH ACCUMULATED WEALTH

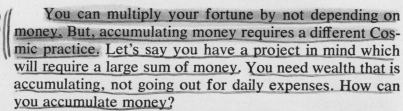

You can multiply your fortune by not depending on money. But, accumulating money requires a different Cosmic practice. Let's say you have a project in mind which will require a large sum of money. You need wealth that is accumulating, not going out for daily expenses. How can you accumulate money?

Money is accumulated not as much by investment and reinvestment as by savings. Money that is saved must earn enough interest to prevent inflation from eroding its value. First budget your own needs. Determine what your financial needs will be to cover the basics:

* Your housing, utilities, and maintenance.
* Your food and clothing, personal needs, cosmetics.
* Health and medical requirements, insurance.
* Transportation, entertainment, and miscellaneous.
* Seed money, speculative money, and fortune multiplier money.
* Savings.

Plan to set aside a small amount each month for savings. Estimate an amount that is comfortable and that you can do with, no matter what emergencies arise. Many people plan to save, but they set their sights a little too high. It is better to plan for a smaller amount that you can afford than to try to make a bigger savings "bite" that you'll have to skip now and then.

Cosmosis activates excellent investment opportunities once you've accumulated a substantial amount of wealth.

Here are some examples of how Cosmosis has brought about favorable opportunities for those who've practiced the prosperity rituals and suggestions in this chapter.

**How Kay Bought
a Profitable Restaurant**

Kay had operated a very successful catering business ever since her husband's death. She made money and she saved it not for a rainy day but for the Cosmosis-directed opportunity that she *knew* would present itself to her. Daily, she practiced the Kundalini breathing and meditation exercise described in Chapter 1.

One day, out of the blue, without any warning, a customer of hers told her that she was selling her restaurant to move to a warmer climate. She offered to sell it to Kay, explaining that the manager of the business would stay on to help her run it since she didn't know much about it.

Kay submitted the question during her use of the speculation technique mentioned in this chapter and she was guided to purchase the business.

Within a year's time she was making money hand-over-fist. She was making more than the previous owner!

Today, Kay owns three restaurants and has disposed of the catering business. Her personal income has risen by more than 300 per cent in about four years' time. Kay had a Cosmic inundation of wealth as a consequence of saving for the inevitable wealth that was to be hers! With Cosmosis and the higher intelligence working for her, nothing could stop her in her climb to the top. She is still prospering and she is saving anew. The forces themselves only know the next wonderful phase which will be opened to her. She may double or triple her accumulated wealth with the next step which she will be guided into—she tapped Cosmic energy and used it.

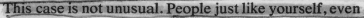

This case is not unusual. People just like yourself, even

those with as little as a few hundred extra dollars, have been able to make fortunes. It is not impossible when you open up to the infinite storehouse which can be yours.

How Leonard Used His Savings
to Move to a Better Job

Leonard W. represents a case of Cosmosis direction that defies routine explanation. Leonard had been saving for years. His weekly paycheck always had "seed money" and some extra cash—a very small amount—for his Cosmosis multiplication. He always called it his "nest egg" for emergencies, but he knew within himself somewhere that it would be more than that.

A skilled mechanic, Leonard's take-home pay from a small garage was not much. He and his wife had the necessities, but not much more.

He, too, was using the prosperity ritual and the Fortune Multiplier technique, asking that he might be led to do the right thing with the accumulated wealth.

His opportunity came when a representative of a large oil company offered to sell him a franchise to a gasoline station in a good location at the intersection of two heavily traveled highways.

Leonard got the Cosmic "go ahead" and used his accumulated wealth to buy the franchise. It has been paying big dividends ever since. Leonard is happier, too, with his own small business. He is his own boss and his customers take readily to his smile and easygoing manner.

How Seed Money Came Back
When It Was Needed

Cliff R. was a manager in the home office of a large corporation. He had been generous all his life and had given

106

large sums of money to charitable causes. But in his late fifties, he became an alcoholic and lost his responsible position.

His wife had died a few years earlier, but his son and daughter-in-law were willing to give him a room in which to live while he attended the Alcoholics Anonymous meetings.

It took him a long time to recover his self-confidence and overcome his dependence on alcohol. But as he was going through his readjustment, he was never short of cash to meet his obligations. Old friends remembered how he gave lovingly and freely when he was in a strong financial position. They offered, voluntarily, to help him here and there, with rent, money for gasoline, cash for needed clothing, etc. Within a year's time, Cliff was employed again and earning his way in the world—without alcohol. The seed money he had given out came back when he needed it.

The law of cause and effect, or Karma, explains this returning of the seed money. What we *give* automatically cycles back into what we *receive*. As has been shown in earlier chapters, this is the same law that affects the thoughts and feelings which we send out. Everything we think, say, or do becomes Cosmically attached to other vibrations of a similar character, until a "vibrational network" is formed which *returns* the vibrations to the *sender* in different forms.

THE FINANCIAL LAW OF KARMA
THAT HAS NEVER FAILED
THROUGHOUT THE AGES

The Karmic effect of *giving* works with seed actions and thoughts, too. Try giving of yourself in forms other than money and you will be rewarded at another time when you need it. Give a "thank you" to a loved one, give some encouragement to a friend who is "down in the dumps."

Offer a friendly smile to a stranger. Offer your volunteer time to a hospital, orphanage, or other charity.

Your life will be inspired, your energies renewed and revitalized by any project you take on which benefits, uplifts, or helps others. Be careful not to do these things in order to be rewarded. Do not look for immediate personal dividends. Simply accept them when they come.

Money is just another form of spiritual or psychic substance. It is not an end in itself but a means of accomplishing the highest good—or the lowest evil. It can be used for your fulfillment or it can be your undoing. Your own motivation, your goals, your willingness to be a Cosmic servant will determine how you use money—or how it uses you.

How Jess Made His First Fortune in Las Vegas

Jess took the small amount of accumulated wealth that he had and went to Las Vegas. Much of his life was devoted to helping others. The trip to Las Vegas was one of the first really big vacations that he had allowed himself. It was a luxury for him which he felt he owed himself. Besides, he was a bachelor and could afford to spend more on this trip than a man with a family to take care of.

He had set aside a few thousand dollars with which to gamble. Jess was not ordinarily a compulsive gambler and did not gamble frequently when he was at home.

His several thousand dollars multiplied over and over during his two-week stay and special arrangements had to be made to transfer his winnings to his hometown bank.

Jess let himself be led by Cosmosis—he was free to speculate and take risks. He did not force Cosmosis to help, but turned his entire being over to Cosmosis for guidance and direction. Slowly, quietly, surely, the impressions came to him. He was an instrument of the greater powers of the universe.

Being aware of Karma, Jess gave some of his fantastic winnings to worthy causes as seed money. The cycle completed itself for him. The Karmic pattern will continue to reap profitable circumstances for Jess. In one form or another, his seed money is still manifesting itself—another fortune is "in the making." Let his money success fire you with ambition to do the same.

ints to Remember from This Chapter

1. The first step in attracting, holding, and multiplying money is to get rid of your guilt about being rich.

2. Your ability to meet a need plus the demand for the need will equal your ability to make money.

3. A wealth-producing money consciousness manifests itself when we lose our fear of money.

4. The Cosmosis Fortune Multiplier technique is to use money but not to depend on it.

5. Accumulated wealth, or savings, will give you the extra leverage to move up to a higher financial status.

Chapter 7

HOW COSMOSIS CAN MAKE YOU POPULAR AND ATTRACTIVE

Why are people drawn to each other by seemingly hidden forces? What magnetism and personal charm is instantly recognized as appealing? Why are some people attracted to certain "types" of people?

The Cosmic explanation for popularity and human attraction is unfolded, for the first time, in this chapter. With frankness and candor, you'll learn the magic keys to beauty. With these keys you'll become more radiant, more sought-after, more appealing to the opposite sex than you've ever been. Cosmosis will help you bring out the inner glow of youth and health. It will change your personality into a forceful, yet loving, magnet that will draw other people to you. With a Cosmosis-energized personality, people will literally want to be close to you because of your attractive *auric vibration.*

WHAT IS THE TRUE BASIS OF LASTING POPULARITY?

People are attracted to other people because of the

natural complement of their attractive vibrations or auric fields of harmonious energy. This vital life vibration is related to sexual attraction or the desire to continue life. We are attracted to the people whom we feel, Cosmically, could combine vibrationally with us to form another life. Popularity is related to our survival instinct.

Cosmic energy supplies the auric vibration that others are attracted to. Lasting popularity exists when a person's supply of Cosmic energy is continuous. If the Cosmic energy level goes down, popularity goes down with it.

Public personalities who realize this secret make certain that they do not appear in public unless they are in top form, energy level high and all mental and spiritual systems *ready to go!* From actors and actresses to political and social leaders, all exhibit unlimited energy and zest for living.

A CHECKLIST FOR KEEPING
YOUR COSMIC ENERGY LEVEL UP

Here are some essential basic suggestions for keeping your energy level up for attractiveness when you are meeting new people or when you are dealing with old friends under special circumstances:

1. Be sure to eat regular, balanced meals, get plenty of sleep, fresh air, and exercise. Psychic health begins with good physical and mental health.

2. When you know you are in for a trying occasion, gear yourself for the worst by preparing yourself to be calm and confident *before* you are into the situation. Sit quietly for the Kundalini attunement mentioned in Chapter 1. Let God's psychic force work through your actions.

3. You may have friends who "draw" energy from you.

When you are in the presence of these people, make sure that they are not trying to force you to give more than you should be giving.

4. Place yourself in situations which can be renewing and regenerating. Some people find vacations are helpful. Others need to be near bodies of water, open rivers, lakes, the seaside. You may be the type that does well in mountainous areas where you can feel close to nature.

5. Schedule "quiet time" when you can be alone, to meditate and feel Cosmosis flowing through your body and mind. Don't let yourself use the "leftover" time for quietness. Do make a point of preparing yourself for it and setting aside time for reflection and deep thought.

6. Make sure that your personal life, particularly your marriage or love life, does not interfere with your "quiet time"—to the extent that you cannot concentrate, or be alone, or receive the Cosmic directions which may come your way.

7. Be sure to practice the regimen which is described next to increase your Cosmic energy level for a pleasing, attractive personality.

THE REGIMEN FOR INCREASING YOUR COSMIC ENERGY LEVEL

Here is the method for increasing your Cosmic energy level through Cosmic attunement meditation. (This meditation method is more fully explained in my book *The Power of Psychic Awareness,* Parker Publishing Company, Inc., West Nyack, New York.)

1. *Sit in Meditation, Relax, and Repel All Negative Thoughts from Your Mind.* Actually see these negative thoughts going to another location far, far away from you.

2. *Create a Positive Scene in Your Mind's Eye That You*

113

Have a Favorable Reaction To. See yourself in a restful, wooded area, near a lake or beside the ocean. Use any scene or situation that has a positive reaction for you.

3. *Place Your Entire Mind and Body into Neutral.* Let yourself float on the surface of your thoughts. Don't force thought-forms or concentrate on anything. Just let the Cosmic energy fill your entire mind and body with health-giving vitality.

How Ruth Increased Her Energy Level and Found New Friends

Ruth was what some people would call a lackluster person. She complained of being tired, uneasy, or out-of-sorts with herself. A stenographer with a small insurance firm, Ruth was not the person in her office that people rushed up to and talked with because she always had an ache or pain.

Her outlook was so negative that she was often led to gossip about her co-workers.

Ruth had been taking vitamins, food supplements, and nursing one emotional problem after another.

Ruth started to use the regimen for increasing her Cosmic energy level and within three weeks she felt better, she was sleeping well, eating well, and her outlook was turning into one of optimism. One month later she was cheerful at work, she had a ready smile, offered to help when she could, and she stopped gossiping.

"Cosmic energy has done so much for me. I can actually feel it within me," she said. "When you are down, you don't realize how far you've gone until something like this brings you back to normal and gives you a totally new outlook."

Her enthusiasm was so great that she got others in her office into a meditation group with her. The best part of this case history is that the entire office is doing very well. Business is booming and everyone is perking right along.

How Max "Turned On" with Cosmic Energy
and Gave Up Drugs

Max was an 18-year-old high school student studying printing. He was active with the usual pursuits for his age, including improving his secondhand car, dating his favorite girl, and working part time in a local grocery store.

Max had been using some milder drugs for about a year when he was introduced to Cosmic energy meditation by Sandra, a girl in his school who was interested in astrology.

Cosmic attunement had an astounding effect on Max. He felt the inrushing of the higher influences at the very first session with Sandra and her friends. This single experience was enough to change the entire course of his life. He is meditating regularly and he has given up his dependency on drugs. More than his own salvation is at stake, because he is now able to help turn others onto the higher levels of Cosmic awareness and lead them away from drugs.

Max has become more integrated and popular. The real transformation was his ability to relate to the world and himself without drugs.

HOW TO CREATE
LIFELONG FRIENDSHIPS

Lifelong friendships are rare indeed. That's because when you begin to relate deeply to someone, there are bound to be ups and downs, pleasant and unpleasant periods. It seems easier to end a difficult relationship than to continue on with one that is completely unhealthy. But even the most healthy friendships have conflict in them when there is real *relating,* deep acceptance and under-standing. Acceptance of someone else's total being requires a high degree of tolerance for that person's faults and shortcomings. It also requires the ability to be nondefensive about another person's behavior or attitude. Other people have a way of unsettling our ego mechanism or throwing us off-balance. If we are strong and stable, we cannot be threatened by another person's actions or reactions toward us.

The mystical and psychical way of life is not rigid or judgemental. That is, Cosmosis gives you many avenues, and opens you up to a creative and expanding awareness of life's intricacies and interrelationships. This, in turn, makes you more tolerant of others and more loving. If we view friends as threats or if we "use" them because of our own psychological needs, we are not really giving and relating. In these cases, chances are we will not make lifelong friends.

Let's see what the profile of a Cosmosis-directed person is like and how this profile—or way of looking at life—makes it possible to relate to people in a way that creates lifelong friendships.

THE PERSONALITY PROFILE
OF A COSMOSIS-DIRECTED PERSON

1. *The Cosmosis-Directed Person Is Nonjudgemental.* Hold your judgement of people in reserve until you have an opportunity to know them thoroughly. Don't be quick to classify, to condemn, or to "erase" people from your thinking. Often people act out of deep inner needs and they are not always logical or reasonable. They are ruled by feelings, emotions, fears, and desires. They may not always like you, but they may be able to accept you on their terms if you will let them.

2. *The Cosmosis-Directed Person Feels the Unity of All Creation.* Feel the underlying Cosmic connection between your life-force and the life-force in all of nature. Sense your relationship to everything and everybody that you encounter. The same divine aspect that impels you

116

through life also impels others. At first you may be able to feel kinship with other people. But as you grow spiritually, you will feel kinship with all *things,*—all *forms* of life.

3. *The Cosmosis-Directed Person Has a Tolerance for Ambiguity.* Since you are open to universal direction, you will not quickly categorize experiences automatically as "good" or "bad." Much will remain neutral until its final meaning can be arrived at. You will not avoid experiences because they might be unpleasant. Instead, you will welcome each opportunity to know what life is and how it operates. You will not panic if the meaning of a situation is not clear right away. You will let things work through you and around you.

4. *The Cosmosis-Directed Person Is Aware of Spiritual Realities.* Make decisions and take actions based on what is intuitively true for you. Work with your inner feelings, poetic logic, rather than external circumstances and rational logic. Reality is not words nor is it composed of verbal explanations. Reality is moving, changing, growing all the time. There is a spiritual form of reality which intersects our physical world and participates in it.

5. *The Cosmosis-Directed Person Feels That Life Is Sacred.* Peace, love, and brotherhood are major concerns. Let your actions and thoughts radiate the profound and sacred nature of life. Be positive about the Infinite plan for everyone. Harm no person except in self-defense. Spread the light of your understanding of life's deepest meaning. In conversation and in all of your contacts with others be the kind of person you would like to have as a friend.

HOW YOUR COSMOSIS-DIRECTED PERSONALITY WILL AFFECT STRANGERS

If you develop a Cosmosis-directed personality, strangers will not think of you as a "threat." They will not be defensive toward you. You'll find them open, loving,

117

receptive to you and your ideas. You will appear to be different and you'll probably find that people will describe you as "interesting." Cosmosis direction can open up additional doorways to a new life.

Mike N. was an industrial film producer and actor. He owned a small film-producing organization which made films for companies that didn't have the talent or facilities to do their own. He was an excellent craftsman. But he had trouble attracting new clients because people were not favorably impressed with him at first meeting. He just could not sell himself well. As soon as Mike consciously began to direct his personality with Cosmosis, he became more outgoing. People responded to him favorably and he got several new accounts.

Isabel A. owned a gift shop. It was going well because she was buying the things her customers wanted. She could sense the need for products her customers would buy. Her merchandise was unusual. It was priced reasonably. But Isabel's sales volume doubled the year following her use of Cosmosis. She worked diligently to use the personality direction advocated here. It was an enormous plus for her.

Rose D. was a teen-age girl who was lonely, shy, unable to attract friends. Boys ignored her and girls were a little afraid of her since she was a good student. Rose adopted our entire program as her personal development guide and things really began to open up for her. She practiced sincerely and honestly all of the steps outlined in this book.

When Rose manifested Cosmosis in her personality, isolation from friends dissolved. She was outgoing, warm, friendly, and she became a member of a small group of school leaders. She wasn't looked upon as odd or different. Instead, she was accepted and appreciated for what she had become. She began dating boys and within a few months was going steady. For Rose, Cosmosis turned life from a

118

nightmare into a pleasant experience. Each day she now has something to look forward to. She is relaxed, happy, and contented with her life. She is a walking case of "before and after." She is making and keeping friends, many of whom may be with her for a lifetime.

HOW TO TURN YOUR WORST ENEMIES INTO ENTHUSIASTIC FRIENDS

There are several classical ways to deal with enemies. One way is to ignore them. Another is to join them. You can fight them—or, you can change them into *friends* with Cosmosis.

Here is how you can turn enemies into enthusiastic supporters:

1. First determine who your enemies are, why they are against you, or what you are doing, and decide if the people you have listed should be converted into friends. Some of those who are your enemies should stay out of your life. But some should be friendly toward you. Make sure you do not try to convert someone who is trying to destroy you, your reputation, or character. Do not include for conversion anyone who is basically malicious.

2. Once you've developed a list of those whom you've decided to convert to good friends, you are ready to use Cosmosis to bring about the change.

3. Your first step is to maintain your practice of the Kundalini exercise of meditation described in Chapter 1. Next, review the characteristics of the Cosmosis-directed personality in this chapter. Finally, you are ready to adopt a program designed to change each one of your enemies into friends.

4. Spend some time each day in silent meditation for *each* person on your list. See love and harmony surrounding each person. Visualize yourself saying or doing something

119

loving and friendly toward each one. As you picture yourself doing this, make a resolution that you will execute such a friendly action or make an outgoing, loving gesture at your next meeting. Dispel all thoughts that the person is your enemy. Dissolve all negation in your mind which you hold concerning each person.

5. If an unintentional disagreement is preventing you from communicating with each other, take whatever steps are necessary to patch things up. Apologize if necessary. Or, go out of your way to show that all is forgiven.

6. After you've followed the suggestions in steps 4 and 5, you can invoke the Cosmosis energy to bring friendship about. Make certain deep within your own heart that you want to make each person a friend because you are able to see the good potential in him. Don't take this final step unless you feel that you could be a true friend. If you take an attitude of "it's better to have this person as a friend than an enemy" don't proceed. You should go ahead only if you feel that you can extend some trust and real concern for the person or persons on your list.

7. Prepare yourself through meditation and silent prayer. *You are ready to cement friendship with a promise and pact with the higher powers of the universe.* Using the religious, mystical, or psychical symbol that is most sacred to you, swear that you will be a friend to (name each person separately) *forever.* Ask that you be shown the same friendship and give thanks for the activation of this great Cosmosis law. Your "friendship forever pact" will speed the change as long as you continue to practice the other Cosmosis suggestions given to you here.

If you find it necessary to go back on your promise for your own defense or because you find out later that a person cannot be your friend, *you can only reverse this law by severing your ties with that person completely.* All communication, all thought, all actions must be without that person. If your business or social life puts you in touch with

120

the person *in any way*, then it is impossible to reverse this law. This is a Cosmosis law which cannot be taken lightly. You must cut off all contact, all conversation, all thoughts about this person.

The benefits of this practice have been far-reaching in the lives of our Cosmosis students.

How Darlene Made a Friend of Her Mother-in-Law

Darlene, age 22, had a problem with her mother-in-law even before she was married. But after the wedding, it seemed that she and her husband's mother were at opposite ends of every question.

Darlene got into an argument with her mother-in-law about a new house that she and her husband were thinking about buying. It was a lovely bungalow in the suburbs. Her mother-in-law maintained that they were too young and could not afford the investment.

Rather than argue about the matter, Darlene decided to make a friend of her mother-in-law by making a pact with the higher powers. Each day she swore that she would be a good friend, forever.

Her mother-in-law had a habit of telephoning Darlene several times a week. As soon as Darlene answered the telephone and heard the familiar voice, she was reminded of her pact with the higher powers. Darlene visualized love and harmony around herself and her caller. Darlene's responses to her mother-in-law were activated in the direction of total love rather than fear and hatred. At first her new relatedness caught her mother-in-law by surprise. Then she began to be less defensive, more open, more appreciative of Darlene. Within a month, Darlene had captured complete approval from her husband's mother. Six weeks after she had made the pact, the mother-in-law offered to give her son the down payment on the new house.

How Brian Made a Friend
of His Boss

Brian worked as a security guard for a steamship company. A retiree, he worked only part time on the night shift checking the docks to make certain that the ships and warehouses were safe. However, Brian's boss had the instinctive feeling that Brian was not as alert as he should be.

His reliability was not being questioned but his perceptiveness and courage were. Brian had not missed anything while he was making his rounds. He was a good security guard—strong, perceptive, and dedicated to doing a good job. The problem was really a personality clash. So Brian made his pact with the higher powers. Visualizing sincerity and harmony around his boss, he daily reminded himself of his promise to make this man a lifetime friend.

Only two weeks after he made his pact, Brian received the first compliment from his boss. "You did a fine job in spotting the unlocked door to our warehouse last week. A gang of thieves has been operating on the waterfront, and the police realized that our premises might be the next to be burglarized. During your night off, the men were arrested while they were trying to get in the very door you reported. Thanks a lot! We are giving you a raise, and you'll be under consideration for a special merit award from our president."

Brian's boss really liked him. He was sincere in his thanks and always took time out to inquire about Brian's health and his off-the-job life from that moment on. Some time later, Brian was invited to his boss's home for Christmas dinner, since he was alone except for his only daughter who lived many miles away in another city. Shortly after that, Brian received a promotion to supervisor.

HOW TO ENCOURAGE PEOPLE
TO ACCEPT YOUR FRIENDSHIP

Have you ever wanted to be a friend to someone who refused you? It might have happened because your offer was not understood. Your friendship might have represented an ego threat to that person. There are many reasons for refusing friendship. But most boil down to *what does your friendship require?* What emotional price does your friendship exact? What do you expect in return? Do you "trap" a person into being a friend and then expect payment which is more than your friend can give?

Friendship is a give-and-take proposition. The "give" and the "take" must be spontaneous, natural, a response which just happens. Real friendship grows as trust grows. You can't keep an account book on friendship and expect spontaneous concern, love, or trust. It's got to flow from the heart, not the mind. Lasting friendships are built on solid foundations of giving. They are recorded in an eternal record book, not in a checkbook. They are built on mutual needs, not on mutual manipulation. Try forcing a friendship and you've ended one. Any honest, worthwhile person will be your friend if:

1. You do not expect repayment for favors extended.
2. You do not try to coerce, manipulate, or threaten.
3. You will mind your own business.
4. You will give of yourself freely.
5. You will take only what is given freely.
6. You can accept faults, slights, and shortcomings.
7. You do not expect too much.

123

8. You will place your friendship above self and self-needs.
9. You will let things develop naturally.
10. You do not force yourself on anyone who doesn't like you.

This last point is the most important. Don't force your friendship on *anyone.* Let it develop. You will be guided to do and say the right things if you'll let the natural things happen. Above all don't try to stop honesty, sharing, or giving. Present yourself as you are. Don't hide your faults or gloss over a weakness. You'd be surprised at the number of people who will admire you for facing up to *all* that you are.

Cosmosis, the all-pervading energy of the universe, is in your vibration. When you are relaxed and secure in your relationship to others, your vibration is attracted to those who complement it. If you do not let the *natural* force of Cosmosis operate in your relationships, you may find yourself attracted to vibrations which are discordant to yours. The methods and techniques outlined in this self-improvement book are designed to help you discover nature's way to live. All that you do, think, or act upon can be in harmony with the Cosmos. Every step of your life can be guided and directed by the forces of nature. Once you know how to place yourself into the hands of the greater Cosmic plan, you will find every aspect of your life is fulfilling, exciting, and promising.

Becoming a Cosmic instrument will bring you friends—understanding, lovable friends—who will travel the earth journey with you. Your personality will attract the people you need.

You are not alone.

Your destiny is what you make it—with Cosmosis.

The next chapter shows you how to be young and healthy with the aid of Cosmosis. Let's keep going and build the life-style and improvement program that will make your life challenging and rewarding.

POINTS TO REMEMBER FROM THIS CHAPTER

1. We are attracted to people whose vibrations, or magnetic fields, are complementary to ours.

2. Your personality can be magnetic if you keep your Cosmic energy level up. Quiet meditation is the best way to renew this energy.

3. The Cosmosis-directed personality is non-judgemental, feels the unity of all creation, has a tolerance for ambiguity, is aware of spiritual realities, and looks upon life as sacred.

4. You can turn enemies into friends by visualizing love and harmony around them and by promising the higher powers of the universe that you will be friends forever.

5. People will accept your friendship if you give and take naturally, spontaneously, and without forcing yourself.

Chapter 8

HOW COSMOSIS HELPS
TO IMPROVE YOUR HEALTH

Good health helps you tap and use Cosmosis. And Cosmosis energy can assist you in getting and keeping good health. That's why we have this chapter on physical and mental well-being. Any self-improvement program would be incomplete without the vital information you will get here. Everything you've learned up to this point about the universal laws guiding the universe and your life will help you look and feel years younger than you are. The health problems usually associated with aging can be overcome, halted, or slowed down with Cosmosis.

WHAT MAKES PEOPLE AGE?

Middle age begins at about 26 years. Old age can set in any time after that. The question is: Why do some people look vibrant and attractive at every age? What is their secret? Isn't it natural to become old? Yes, it is natural to grow through the passage of time. But it isn't natural to be tired, apathetic, or rundown. *How* we grow depends on

127

life-style—the total *way* we live through the years. Cosmosis points the way to a healthy life.

The two most important factors in leading a healthy life are: (1) maintaining a high degree of energy, and (2) prolonging motivation to do things, to find life challenging and interesting. These two factors affect the kind of lifestyle we adopt. Without zest and desire, our living patterns can become flabby, out-of-shape, or self-destructive. We age. In other words, our mental and physical style affects the environment we choose. That environment can be healthy instead of destructive. When our life-style is guided by Cosmosis, we live in a fountain of youth because we have the energy and outlook of a young person.

People age because of:

1. Emotional stress, upset, and worry.
2. Poor diet and nutrition.
3. Polluted and poisoned air, water, and food.
4. Recurrent infections.
5. Accidents.
6. Ignorance of hygiene and self-care.
7. Detrimental life-styles.

HOW CAN AGING BE SLOWED AND REVERSED?

Ivan R. was a retiree in his sixties. He'd worked for a bank. During his retirement, he took a part-time job as a clerk for an accounting firm. Ivan found time to become interested in the deeper spiritual principles of the universe and wrote to me about his investigations of psychic phenomena.

We carried on a lively correspondence concerning the subject of mediumship.

He spoke in one of his letters about the infusion of energy he often felt when he was sitting in seances. "Sometimes I feel cool breezes and then a great tide of warmth wells up within me," he said. "Renewed strength stays with me for days. I wish I could have that feeling all the time.

"My physical self needs more stamina and zest, too. Do you have any recommendations?"

I wrote to Ivan and suggested that he try adjusting his life-style. Here's what I recommended:

1. *Care for the Physical Self.* A balanced diet with large amounts of protein, attention to all the vitamin needs, and a reduction of fat and caloric intake is the beginning of physical care. Regular elimination of wastes and regularly scheduled rests are musts. Finally, exercise and recreation should be included to keep the body and mind working smoothly.

2. *Care for the Mental Self.* Emotional stress can be avoided by not putting one's self into a position where tense circumstances are likely to develop. A good sense of humor can rescue you from the inability to function as a result of excess emotional strain. Love of family and friends improves attitudes and so does active involvement in projects and activities with other people.

3. *Care for the Spiritual Self.* "Widen your horizon" is the key idea here. Life can be an exciting event when we look for new things to do and novel subjects to learn about. Knowledge and experience in spiritual matters help to broaden our basis for living. A healthy life-style includes room for inventiveness, new ideas, new people, and new points of view. Cosmosis gives us a creative and revitalizing life-style.

129

Ivan R. put into practice our recommended plan to slow and reverse the aging process. He found people interesting and the world became a more fascinating place in which to live. This attitude affected his mental and emotional self. He simply avoided negative circumstances by refusing to energize them with his time or attention.

Ivan's attention to his physical self dramatized his ability to slow and reverse the aging process.

His physical health was transformed. He not only felt better but looked ten times better. His skin became a healthy color, his muscles were responsive. He looked rested and "on top" of everything. His body organs were working perfectly.

Ivan's case proved that good health can be maintained by this simple plan. He continued to be healthy, happy, and filled with a high motivation to continue enjoying life. He had slowed and reversed the aging process.

Physical aging begins when deficiencies develop because of poor diet and poor assimilation of food. These deficiencies show up in the blood when the supply of nutrient drops. This affects the tissues of the organs because they are not being "fed" properly. After prolonged "malnutrition" of the organs, recognizable symptoms develop.

THE NUTRITIONAL KEYS
TO THE VIGOR OF YOUTH

Not all diseases are caused by germs, viruses, or bacteria. Overall resistance to these invaders can be raised by a carefully planned intake of food.

Repair of the basic building blocks of our bodies, the cells, can easily be complete and continuous. The long-term effort brings the result. At first you'll only feel better now and then. But, if you stay with it, you'll build natural resistance to disease. You'll feel better 100 per cent of the time. Continuous good health will electrify your body with the vigor of real youth. Here are the nutritional keys.

Start by watching nature, by taking food in its most natural state. Uncooked fruits and vegetables are excellent for you. Appetite for specified food is not a reliable way to eat. Some foods such as coffee, salt, alcohol, sugar, and carbohydrates increase appetite for them. They are, in a sense, habit-forming. The more you eat, the more you want.

Freezing takes the vitamin-mineral and enzyme potency away from food. So try to buy food when it's fresh. Avoid foods with a long shelf life in the store or in your cupboard.

You'll also want to avoid food which has been enriched, refined, or artificially preserved. Labeling law requires that foods of this kind bear a note indicating that the contents of the package have been treated or exposed to additives, sprays, colorings, antibiotics, pesticides, and so forth.

Beware of food that has been picked green for shipment to your locality.

A QUICK LOOK
AT THE VITAMIN ESSENTIALS

Virginia W. was overweight. She looked 20 years older than her age. It embarrassed her and she found herself making little apologies for herself when she was in the presence of friends. She knew that the sheer volume of food she ate was out of line. And, she knew all about the desirability of eating less. But she was uncertain about vitamins. "I know what I should *not* eat," she said, "but I don't know what I *should* eat. I'm planning to reduce slowly. I want to lose about 40 pounds. What vitamins are necessary to good health? And what foods should be included in my diet?"

I gave Virginia a quick look at the vitamin essentials so she could plan her menus. She had set a tough goal for herself—slow reduction of weight. Realizing the danger of crash diets, drugs, and other inducements to "do it all at once," she was determined to take her pounds off sensibly and keep them off.

Here is the recommended daily requirement for an average adult in good health (most supplemental vitamin capsules contain this dosage):

*10,000 international units of Vitamin A.

*2 milligrams of Vitamin B-1.

*3 milligrams of Vitamin B-2.

*24 milligrams of niacin.

*150 milligrams of Vitamin C.

*400 international units of Vitamin D.

*140 grams of animal protein.

*1,000 milligrams of calcium.

*500 milligrams of phosphorous.

*18 milligrams of iron.

*150 micrograms of iodine.

Here are the common sources of supplemental vitamins. Your physician can help you find the proper amounts for you.

*Vitamin A—colored vegetables, cod liver oil, eggs, liver.
*Vitamin B—liver, wheat germ, yogurt, brewer's yeast,
    (Complex) whole grains, sprouts.
*Vitamin C—raw whole orange, bioflavonoid capsules,
    ascorbic acid, sprouted seeds.

Vitamin D—cod liver oil, sunshine, bone-meal tablets.

Vitamin E—wheat germ.

Vitamin F—lecithin granules.

Vitamin K—green, leafy vegetables.

Calcium—milk, natural cheese, turnip greens, bone meal.

Phosphorous—wheat germ, milk, natural cheese, egg yolk.

Iron—parsley, beef liver, molasses.

On a daily basis, Virginia planned her menus with the help of the following program:

1. *Some milk* each day.
2. *Two or more servings* of meat, such as beef, veal, pork, lamb, poultry, fish, or eggs. (Alternatives could be dry beans, dry peas, or nuts.)
3. *Four or more servings* of one of the following—a citrus fruit, a dark-green or deep-yellow vegetable, other vegetables or fruits including potatoes.
4. *Four or more servings* of bread or cereal made from whole grain. (Alternatives can be enriched or restored.)

Within two months, Virginia began to look much better. She took small portions of food but didn't make herself consciously aware of calories. She just ate less, balancing her diet with the essential vitamins and minerals. Within four months, Virginia had lost 40 pounds and looked years younger. Her skin was a radiant glow; her hair and eyes looked healthy and vibrant.

Her Cosmosis life-style helped her stick to the diet.

She was no longer apologetic and people loved to be with her.

Her outlook on life was thrilling. She was inquisitive and full of exuberance. She was a very attractive person who seemed years and years younger. "I just can't fully realize what has happened to me," she said later. "So many wonderful things have happened. Life couldn't be better. I have to pinch myself every morning when I get up just to remind myself that I'm alive. It's such a great feeling to have things go in my favor for a change. I must be the luckiest person in the world."

WHAT WILL MAKE ANYONE OLD
AHEAD OF SCHEDULE ?

There is one way to get old before your time: think about death; think about the boredom of it all.

Thought is a substantial thing that affects your health directly. Reversing the aging process is a matter of thinking about the opposite of death, disease, lack, or boredom. The fountain of youth is in your state of consciousness. You can carry youth with you in your thoughts. Cosmosis helps us to attract what we think.

The fountain of youth is brought into your consciousness by thought. It is transferred into youthful activities and youthful appearance.

Jim was a college student in his twenties. He was young in years. But his thoughts were those of a man many years older. Everything was wrong with the world. To Jim, life was not a liberating experience. He unconsciously looked forward to death even at his age.

Jim was undecided about what to study. His life's vocation hadn't hit him yet. He was studying a liberal arts course until he could "make up his mind." He was in an emotionally depressed state. "I wish I could pull out of it but I can't," he confessed. "Everything seems so tired and dull, and it all seems so useless."

"Can you try looking for the excitement in your life?" I asked. "Can you look for the novel, the different, the unusual, the unexpected? Can you let yourself reflect the best that life has to offer?"

We had several sessions together, in which we searched for the interesting aspects of Jim's life. He used the Kundalini formula explained in Chapter 1.

As time passed, we located the positive elements. Jim found out that his life was liberating.

He selected history as his major academic field. He also "selected" a young lady who appealed to him very much, too. The following year they were married.

His state of psychic consciousness made it all possible. By looking at life as an exciting event, it became meaningful for him. His outlook changed. Then, everything that happened "to" him changed too. He put himself into a youthful state of consciousness.

THE SUBCONSCIOUS FOUNTAIN OF YOUTH

Each of us is guided and directed by the ideas that we let our subconscious dwell on. Our subconscious mind is our silent partner for good or ill. When we tell it that we want to live, life is a series of exciting, rewarding events. We are activating the deepest creative mechanism within us. In fact, you don't even need to consciously believe what you are suggesting to your subconscious mind. It will act on your commands, despite what your conscious mind tries to argue you out of.

Here's a way to direct your silent partner.

Try these *youth commands* each night before you go to bed:

* "I am gaining new vigor, youthfulness, and vitality each day."
* "Life is a wonderful event filled with new, exciting activities."
* "My health and my body organs are perfect."

135

* "I am eternally youthful in mind, body, and consciousness."
* "Youthful thought and action are growing within my subconscious mind."
* "Radiant energy and the will to live are always with me."
* "Everything I do, think, and say is an expression of youth."

Repeating these commands to yourself just a few minutes each evening or morning will accomplish much for you. You are directing your subconscious mind to carry out these directions. The great creative force of the universe will energize these commands and bring them about in your life.

YOUTH AND SEXUAL POTENCY

Sexual proficiency is not related to age.
Sexual enjoyment is not related to age.
Sexual desire is not related to age.
But, sex is related to general health. Emotional factors play a major role in healthy sexual adjustment. Emotional conflict is behind most sex problems related to: (1) impotency in men; (2) frigidity in women; and (3) menopause in men and women.

How Margaret Lived
Through Menopause Successfully

Margaret G. was "the type." Her premenstrual tension changed her into a beast for everyone who had to be near her. Menopause was likely to bring about increased irritability, hot flashes, headaches, and high anxiety.

Margaret G. knew from her own inner awareness that the "change" might be difficult since even her normal periods were emotionally difficult. Natural foods taken during menopause can help ease the nervous tension usual-

136

ly associated with this transition. Menopause does not spell the end of a healthy sex life for a woman. It is a physiological change that is necessary. It does not need to be a major emotional crisis.

Margaret took extra Vitamin A; extra Vitamin B complex, especially brewer's yeast and liver; calcium; Vitamin E and wheat germ; lecithin granules; and Vitamin C. In addition, Margaret G. increased her protein intake and her consumption of organ meats.

She exercised regularly. She meditated and stayed away from emotionally disturbing situations. She followed the simple formula for the fountain of youth that we discussed at the beginning of this chapter.

She began the fountain of youth program as she entered her 33rd year. Menopause began at 37.

She sailed through without any difficulty. In fact, her regular premenstrual tensions lessened considerably about six months after she began the program.

I've recommended the same natural method of renewing the body and mind to others. In case after case, it has slowed the ordinary age process. In some cases, it has completely reversed the stagnation and dullness usually associated with the middle years.

WHAT FOOD HALTS AGING?

"How can I stop aging right now?" the lady asked. She was over 40, overweight, and overanxious. "Is there a single food I can take which will help me look younger?" she asked frankly.

"Yes there is one 'food' which will do the trick," I answered with a twinkle in my eye. "That food is physical exercise." We laughed together. Physical exercise on a planned basis is the best youth tonic. Of course, it must be adapted to your needs. But most people can walk for extra physical exercise. Many have access to a swimming pool.

Swimming is an excellent way to stay young. Just ten or 15 minutes of calisthenics per day will work wonders. You can even invent your own exercises and still see the fine results of a trim body, active mind, and uplifted spirit.

 There is no single food which will make you young. There is no single exercise that will make you young, either, but if you care for (1) your physical self, (2) your mental self, and (3) your spiritual self, you have found the fountain of youth.

HOW TO AVOID DESTRUCTIVE MEALS

If you eat at home, you have the best control over what you eat and the amount you force into your system. The simplest meals are best. Small portions, which are selected in a way that give you a balanced amount of the vitamins and minerals you need, open the door to continuous bodily health.

But, if you are a frequent guest at the dinner tables of other people, let your friends know you are a "health enthusiast" and cannot eat rich, fattening, or complicated foods. Most people will understand once they know you are really serious about it, and they will give you only what you can handle with ease. Besides, you can always be good company no matter what you eat.

SOME COMMON AILMENTS ASSOCIATED WITH AGING WHICH CAN BE OVERCOME

There are several ailments usually associated with aging that can be overcome, because in many cases these diseases are preventable. Often they have a psychosomatic or emotional cause.

Success for some people is brought about under emotional tension. And with the tension comes the probability of ulcer, colon problems, asthma, and migraine headaches.

Prolonged anxiety shows first of all in the disruption of digestion along the alimentary canal or the esophagus, stomach, small, and large intestine. No wonder "nervous people" have ulcers and colon trouble. Fear, resentment, and anger cause secretion of highly acidic gastric juices and an increased blood supply throughout the alimentary canal. This "acidity" helps induce ulcers and inflame the canal.

Asthma and many other intrinsic allergies are often traced to unwanted and unresolved emotional conflicts deep within the subconscious mind. Asthma is simply a condition during which the muscles in the walls of the bronchioles create an extreme spasm and cause a shortage of air for the lungs. It is usually a progressive disease and can become worse and worse.

Migraine headaches, recurring headaches accompanied by chilliness and "spots" before the eyes, occur when the arteries of the brain are distended. But the cause of the distention is often emotional in origin. That is why complete health includes mental and emotional health and control over one's affairs.

Youth is often thought of as a physical attribute. But the well-balanced, mature person also takes into consideration emotional stability, a factor often absent in youth.

The next chapter discusses the fascinating aspects of mental health surrounding love—nature's greatest wonder drug.

Emotional conflict which brings about "psychosomatic" illness can be overcome by:

1. Identifying the conflict.

2. Taking steps to overcome it.

3. Keeping oneself out of self-destructive circumstances in the future.

Emotional conflict is almost impossible to "face" alone. That is why help is needed. If the situation is deep-seated enough, then professional assistance is required. But often, embarking on a self-improvement program—such as the one outlined in this book—will help establish a way of living which is satisfying and meaningful and will provide a means of dealing with conflict.

The individual who is mentally healthy is able to resolve conflict within himself and tensions between himself and other people. He can appraise situations realistically and is socially responsible for his actions. In other words, he has reduced conflict by finding appropriate outlets for his own basic needs. He is not frustrated in his quest to find meaning in life. In fact, conflict helps him find satisfaction. Although absolute health is an ideal, repeated failure to make suitable adjustments to conflict can result in psychosomatic illness.

POINTS TO REMEMBER FROM THIS CHAPTER

1. People age because of emotional stress; poor nutrition; polluted air, water, and food; recurrent infections; accidents; ignorance of personal hygiene; and detrimental life-styles.

2. Aging can be slowed and reversed through care of the physical self, the mental self, and the spiritual self by applying Cosmosis principles.

3. Vitamins are still the keys to youthful vigor and strength. Daily food intake should provide all the nutrient essentials.

4. "Youth commands" help the subconscious silent partner energize youthful vitality.

5. Sexual fulfillment is not related to age but it is related to general health.

6. Physical exercise is the best youth tonic.

7. Emotional conflicts can cause ulcers, colon problems, asthma, and migraine headaches. A self-improvement program can establish a way of living which provides effective means for dealing with conflict, by applying the principles of Cosmosis to the problem.

Chapter 9

HOW TO CREATE A BETTER
LOVE LIFE WITH COSMOSIS

People certainly do need people. We are all alike in this respect. But not everyone should be married. If you are married, or would like to be, or are going to be, this chapter will be an invaluable aid to you.

Here you'll find out how to find the right lifemate, how to keep your mate, and what to do if you've made the wrong selection or if your marriage is "drooping and sagging."

Cosmosis, the eternal force of the universe, plays a more noticeable role in interpersonal relationships than in any other part of life. It can uplift a marriage, place the partners in perspective to each other, and help sustain love. But, if deep understanding of the universal laws is absent, marriage can turn into a nightmare and drag down every other attempt to build a meaningful life.

THE UNIVERSAL LOVE PRINCIPLE

Our ability to love is dependent on our ability to understand, accept, and love ourselves. At first glance it sounds strange to say that we can only give ourselves in love to another person when we have found love of self, but this is true. We can only love when we have "extra" of it or when we are so concerned about another that we do not need to gratify our own needs. That's the difference between using a person and loving a person. When we use a person, we are accepting only the part or parts which suit us. *When we love someone, we are accepting the whole person because we have enough security in our own "self-love" to give to someone else.*

The universal love principle is this: *the more love we can give, the more love we get.* It's the same Cosmic law which works in other situations. The wealthier we are, the wealthier we are likely to be. The healthier we are, the healthier we are likely to be. That's because when things are headed in a certain direction, chances are they will continue in that direction unless something drastic is done to change matters.

Love is the same way. The more we love ourselves, the more we can love other people, including our lifelong lover We can accept others to the same extent that we can accept ourselves.

If we have trouble in the area of love, it means we are having trouble with our self-concept, our self-love, and that is where Cosmosis can help.

But, let's start at the beginning. How can you find the *right* mate with the help of your Cosmosis way of life?

FINDING YOUR TRUE MATE
THE EASY WAY

Most people choose a husband or wife based on chance, closeness, or availability, rather than on the factors which make for success. Chance means emotion, sometimes raw emotion, which is no basis for building a lasting marriage.

Want to have the cards stacked in your favor? Here is the easy way to find the right mate, the one who can last for your entire life (Let's assume you are following the Cosmosis recommendations outlined in the other chapters of this book.):

1.) *Meditate with the Object in Mind of Being Led to the Right Mate.* This means sitting in silence, free from distractions, communing with the higher forces, letting Cosmosis energy into your vibration and sending out a "Cosmic call" for the *right* one to be sent to you. Do not select the first person who crosses your path or someone you feel "sorry" for. Be suspicious of your emotions if you find yourself "falling" for someone who seems "impossible" for you. Similarities in attitude, life-style, and goals are essential to a lifelong marriage. Finding the areas of similarity takes time, leisure time, time alone from others. It takes exploration of your deepest longings and fears. It takes sharing of your experiences, desires, hopes, and misfortunes. It takes trust and respect.

2.) *Emotional Stability, the Ability to Get Along Smoothly with Other People, Decreases Your Risk Factor.* If you cannot relate well to others, your risk in marrying someone is much higher. Sooner or later your stability, or instability, will surface and affect your marriage and your happiness or unhappiness. If you are trying to escape your maladjustments and conflicts and think that marriage will be a magical solution, you might as well stop right here and plan for divorce.

3.) *How Well You Know Someone Depends on How Long You've Known That Person.* Love often happens at first sight. But marriages that last do not occur overnight. Quick marriages are big risks. The length of time you've known someone is a factor in success or failure. Pretense and deception dissolve in time, and real understanding, or lack of it, reveals itself.

4.) *Common Interests, Goals, and Values Lead to Greater Happiness in Marriage.* Wide differences in background often lead to unexpected unhappiness later on. While a person who is "different" is attractive and mysterious, he or she may try to assert an entirely foreign life-style and attitude over you. Beware of anyone who tries to make you over! This does not mean that you and your spouse need to be the same, but your fundamental outlook and standards, your values and tastes, should be compatible.

5) *Sexual Adjustment and Harmony Is One of the First "Hurdles" of a Lifelong Relationship.* Good sexual adjustment is not a matter of technique. It is a matter of deep emotional responses. These, in turn, are governed by an individual's relationship to the universe and the Cosmic flow of events and energies. Those in a lower level of vibration are likely to have confused, often conflicting, sexual responses. Those who have made attunement with the higher forces, through such self-improvement programs as Cosmosis, usually have healthy sexual and emotional responses in marriage.

How Charles Found the Right Mate

Charles O. was a devoted student of Cosmosis teachings. A widower in his early thirties, he followed the Cosmosis program with the object in mind of being led to the right mate.

Charles met his wife, Charlotte, at a Yoga meeting and they joined the same meditation group. They developed a warm and beautiful friendship. Charles followed our guide to finding your true mate. He and Charlotte met every test! They got married and today are a very happy couple.

How Mae Located Her Husband
Easily and Quickly

Mae W., a stenographer in her twenties, had been looking for a husband for a long time. She was the kind of person whom everyone felt would never be able to find the right man. Yet, within one year after she started letting Cosmosis work for her she was married to an executive. He met all of the criteria above.

Mae started her search with a meditation that she be led to the right man or that the right man be led to her. She actually accepted a promotion to be secretary to this handsome bachelor who became her mate.

Today they have a boy and girl and live comfortably and happily together.

How Barbara Was Led to Her Future Husband

Barbara G. followed the universal love principle and activated her search for a lasting mate. She meditated regularly, and vowed to stress the tests of emotional stability, common interests, and sexual adjustment for any man who became a serious contender. Barbara was in her twenties, a graduate student in economics, and a proficient musician, specializing her talent with the organ.

Actually several men were led to Barbara and she had a difficult time making a selection. She dated them all for awhile until she could apply the tests and receive guidance from the higher realms through her Cosmosis techniques. Slowly she narrowed down to two men, both of whom she found attractive and both of whom appeared to pass the tests. She made her final decision because of two important factors.

One of the men, Roger, appeared to be emotionally immature, was off again and on again, getting into vicious arguments with people, and often tried to drag Barbara down with criticism. Every little thing she did was "dumb" or "stupid" or "selfish." The factor of emotional instability ruled Roger out.

Meanwhile, Bob was ruled into serious consideration

147

because he was taking the time to get to know Barbara through long conversations. They spent periods of time together, enjoying each other, shutting out the world, and just letting themselves "be." Love grew and deepened. Bob was working for his master's degree in English and was scheduled to get it at the same time Barbara got her masters in economics. They both were awarded the degrees and then they were married. They are happy and have adjusted to married life. They have every reason to assume that they'll be together for a lifetime.

HOW TO KEEP A MARRIAGE HAPPY WITH COSMOSIS

When the honeymoon is over, the adjustment period begins. Happiness in marriage exists when the partners merge on all planes of consciousness and all levels of being. Then they become as "one" living entity.

If you are the type to be willful, a strong personality, and expect something from the marriage other than that which your partner expects, you are in for rough periods.

But, if you are able to give as well as take, if you are looking for a depth of understanding and concern, and you express tenderness and try to fulfill your partner's needs, you have a good chance to become happy "as one person."

Cosmosis can help you adapt to your partner, to live through argument and conflict, and adjust to a way of living together which is happy.

Cosmosis is the eternal life energy in all things. Cosmosis teachings, techniques, and methods—which are outlined in this book—are designed to give you lasting control, harmony, and attunement with: (1) your deepest self, (2) the forces of nature and the universe, and (3) the deepest selves you find in other people.

Marriage suddenly puts the "other people" part of you into focus for concentrated attention. The basic Cosmosis techniques can help you share your life with your partner so that your love grows and matures in a healthy way.

The following outlines how you would use the basic Kundalini exercise to assist you in your marriage.

HOW THE KUNDALINI EXERCISE CAN IMPROVE YOUR MARRIAGE

Your marriage partner is more than just another person, a foreign intrusion. Your partner may have started out as "another person" but becomes the "same person" as you. Your partner becomes *part* of you.

The Kundalini exercise can be altered slightly to include the new part of you, your mate. Here is how it can be done.

Use the magic Cosmosis formula as the basis of your metaphysical work to become closer, through love, to your marriage partner.

1. *Regular Breathing.* Sit erect, but comfortably, in a chair. Or you may lie down on a sofa or bed. Close your eyes softly. Allow no distractions. Breathe at your regular rate. Bring air into your lungs. *Hold it for a few seconds.* Discharge it automatically.

2. *Holding the Breath and Focusing the Energy for Love.* As you hold your breath, feel the ionized, Cosmic particles fill your lungs. As you feel the energy flowing throughout your body, see "in your mind's eye" the closeness of your marriage partner. See the etheric double standing before you. Then see this double merging with your own body. Feel your mind and spirit as one. Feel your bodies and feelings as one. Feel your actions, decisions, and realizations as one. *You are one being.* You are loving, caring, feeling as *one body, mind, and soul.*

3. *Riding the Mental Crest of This Cosmic Power.* Once you have focused the energy and feel the above sensations, see the above ideations and thought-forms, simply ride

149

the crest of the power which you have summoned and accumulated.

Relax. Do not force your breathing. Let it return to normal as you are steeped in the love and warm affection of your marriage partner. Be comfortable and wait for the Cosmic impressions of what you should do, if anything, to bring yourself closer into harmony with your partner. Wait for the signals and make a note of them mentally so you can *act* on the Cosmic direction that you get at this time. Solutions to problems and the differences between you will present themselves. You will see how you have made mistakes and you'll be told how to correct them.

The more you perform this magic Cosmosis formula, the more you will benefit. The greatest benefit is the actual metaphysical visualization of your *oneness*. But you can expect additional guidance in the form of impressions as you ride the mental crest of this Cosmic Power. Do not be disappointed if your impressions and direction are not too clear at first. Some days you may not get any specific guidance. On other occasions, many insights and helpful signs will be shown to you.

You are growing together as *one unit,* so it would help you to teach some of these Cosmosis techniques to your partner so that you can perform them together and bring your love into a transcendental, Cosmic purpose. Read this book together and work these techniques and this philosophy into your everyday routine. You will have a life of fulfillment and personal satisfaction if you can both be aware of the universal laws and forces which are guiding our destiny on the earth plane.

How a Marriage Was Kept Happy with Cosmosis

Rick and Mary Ann had been married for 15 years. During that time they had three children. But their relationship was not all peaches and cream. Rick was preoccupied with his contracting firm and Mary Ann had become involved in an endless round of suburban social obligations. Prosperous from all outward appearances, they were nevertheless approaching bankruptcy as far as personal happiness was concerned.

"Sure, we have our usual quarrels about money and how to raise the kids, but it's more than that," Mary Ann tried to explain. "I feel like I'm living with a stranger. Rick works all day. I've got things to do on the weekends and a night or two each week myself. The more successful he becomes, the less love we have. We are practically at the point of meeting only for meals, and even then the children are around. What can we do?"

They were going their own separate ways. Mary Ann was more resentful than Rick. He was just too busy making money to stop and realize what was happening to his marriage.

"You need time together, alone, to re-establish a loving and understanding attitude," I said. "Many people forget that the courtship and early years are spent with just the two of you. You have long periods to dream, explore, to think and plan. Now you've become so absorbed with outside activities and obligations that you've become strangers."

Mary Ann began her "marriage-saving program" with the Cosmosis exercise set out previously in this chapter to help keep her marriage happy. She took it a step further. She was able to explain her dilemma to her husband and Rick also began doing the Cosmosis breathing exercise as described here. In fact, they often took time to do it together!

They both became avid psychic enthusiasts, reading and experimenting on their own initiative. Metaphysical matters became their own private special-interest project. The methods and techniques helped, of course. But, part of this love therapy was the *time* they spent together, much of it alone.

"It's like magic, just as you say," Mary Ann reported to me a few months later. "We are happy and in love. We are building for the future, our future, together, with the help of Cosmosis. Rick is a new man and I guess I'm a new woman. Such a simple thing has made such a big difference."

The case was closed with a happy ending.

WHAT TO DO IF YOU HAVE CHOSEN
THE WRONG MATE

Here is the big question. What should you do if you think you've got the wrong husband or wife? How can you be sure? Can the marriage be salvaged or should it be terminated? How can you avoid self-guilt and malicious psychological and material retaliation?

To put it another way, how can you become a better person through it all?

If your marriage is going sour, with it goes your hopes and dreams, your tenderness, affection, and future happiness. It is a painful experience. Blame is difficult to establish. And, even if you could locate and fix the problems on one person, you or your spouse, it wouldn't bring you back together. It takes two to fall into love and it takes two to fall out of love.

Most marriages are salvageable. Even where infidelity or wandering attentions are involved there is hope.

If you must undergo the adversity of a separation or divorce there is still the human spirit, the desire to triumph and survive, which will ignite within your life. Life as a single person is not all bad. Many people who are single are among society's most productive members.

If you are living the highest life for the highest good,

you are living according to the dictates of Cosmic attunement and awareness. With Cosmosis as your guide and mentor you cannot fail at living, although you may stumble during a single marriage in this particular lifetime.

My final advice, based on the Cosmosis principles recommended in this book, is this: If your marriage won't work, get out of it, and stay away from your former spouse. Don't stick around and try to make life miserable for your mate. Too many lives are ruined by the retaliations of a post-marriage. You cannot force a person into being a convenience for you. Many wives live with their husbands for financial security. Many husbands stay with their wives because of respectability. Such arrangements are self-defeating in terms of the emotional drain and cost of trying to relate to a "former" spouse under such selfish circumstances.

Remember, too, that when you are deeply mired down in turmoil and indecision, it is possible you are not seeing the clear perspective of your marriage. You may need outside help to see what is actually taking place and how you can decide what to do to solve the problem or get out of the marriage. Professional metaphysical and psychic practitioners can help. Most localities have marriage counselors who can give you the perspective you need. A clergyman or noninvolved friend may be able to clear things for you. If you choose a friend to help, be sure the person is not close enough to be involved and can keep his or her mouth closed. You don't want everyone you know to be in on your problems.

COSMOSIS STEPS ON HOW TO END
AN IMPOSSIBLE MARRIAGE

Here are some step-by-step procedures on ending a

153

marriage easily and with the least bitterness when it is impossible to continue the marriage. Don't take these steps until you have definitely decided to end it and you've seen your attorney and started action *that you will not reverse.*

If you are ending a marriage, you need to emphasize the Cosmosis techniques that will help you restore your balance within yourself. You are likely to assume that because you want a divorce or separation there is something "out of kilter" within you. You might even assume more than your share of the blame. Don't! The first thing you'll want to do is:

1. *Relax.* Try to eat balanced meals, sleep regularly, and get plenty of physical exercise.

2. *If There Are Children Involved, Try to Think of Their Welfare and Their Future Development.* Do not think of ways to punish or harm your spouse in order to "get even."

3. *Join an Occult Group and Be Sure to Meditate Each Day to Get the Energy and Guidance You'll Need to Face the Rigors of the Divorce or Separation.* Keep your psychic and metaphysical training going. Nothing can give you as much real solace and peace of mind in a time of crisis. You may find others in your study group who have gone through the same kind of messy divorce action. The understanding and sympathy you'll receive may be just what you need to keep your spirits up and your life going in a positive direction.

4. *Leave Yourself Open to Direction from the Higher Realms of Existence.* Cosmosis direction may have difficulty reaching you if you are overwhelmed by negation, disappointment, or resentment. Set aside meditation time to protect yourself from these blockages. By all means meditate with someone if you need to dissolve hostile and negative feelings and attitudes.

154

5. *Keep in Mind the Central Questions Surrounding Divorce.* Do you now love the person you are married to? Can you live harmoniously with this person? If you get a "no" answer to both of these questions, you have enough reason to impel yourself out of the marriage, immediately.

How Broken Marriages Have Led to Saved Lives

Mrs. F. R. should not have been married in the first place. She was career minded and held a responsible executive position with a large department store. Her husband was resentful of her success in the business world and was jealous of her income. She tried to reach him with all the Cosmosis techniques but failed. She decided on divorce. She is single today—and she is very happy.

Mr. J.B. owned his own import firm and was married to a wife who became frigid. She refused to get help from a marriage counselor or other competent person to deal with this common problem. Mr. J.B. did all he could through the Cosmosis process to help her overcome this problem which at times seemed to abate. Finally, he decided on divorce rather than on constant infidelity. He is divorced, happy, and willing to try marriage to another woman. He read the Cosmic signs correctly and terminated the marriage in time to literally save his life and happiness.

Mrs. B.R. was married to a man who became an alcoholic. He thought of himself only as a heavy drinker or a problem drinker. After trying to get help through Alcoholics Anonymous and using every means she could to re-establish love and understanding, she filed for divorce. Today she is rid of her former husband, working at a job she likes, and maintaining a small house which she loves. She has an active social life and only wishes she could have

155

left her former husband sooner. She might have left him sooner if she had applied the Cosmosis method to receive the guidance she needed.

COSMOSIS ADVICE FOR THOSE WHO ARE ALWAYS SINGLE

As pointed out at the beginning of this chapter, some people should not be married at all. To those who have found themselves in this position, I would like to point out the unique opportunity you have for contributing to the advancement of your fellowman. Many people in the arts, in education, in religion, and in the medical field are single. Even if you do not have a "glamorous" job, you still have extra time and energy which you can devote to helping others find the true meaning of life. You have the unequaled circumstance of being able to make universal attunement spiritually, mentally, emotionally, and physically. You can be an instrument of the Cosmos in a way that others are not able to be. Instead of devoting your life to one person, you can be a friend to many. You have the time to develop a gift or talent. You have the time to find some of the answers that mankind is seeking. You are blessed, maybe without knowing it.

Many of the most fascinating and positive people I know are single. You may be one of those whom God has singled out to live this life in the reflections of man's aspiration. The reason you are single is immaterial. It is what you do with this blessing that counts!

POINTS TO REMEMBER FROM THIS CHAPTER

1. Our ability to extend love depends on the extent to which we love ourselves.

156

2. The universal love principle is that the more love we give, the more love we get.

3. Finding our life-mate the Cosmosis way includes the use of meditation and the tests of emotional stability; the length of time we've known someone; common interests and values; and sexual adjustments based on deep emotional responses.

4. A marriage can be improved by using the Kundalini breathing exercise to become closer to the person you love.

5. A marriage should be ended if love is not the basis of it. Some people are much more happy being single because it gives them a unique opportunity to help others, to develop a talent or gift, and to explore the questions of man's existence.

Chapter 10

HOW TO USE COSMOSIS
FOR GREATER HAPPINESS

All human beings have one thing in common. We are all searching for or trying to maintain happiness. Some of us find it and keep it. Others never quite locate it.

This chapter is about happiness and how to make a few Cosmic adjustments that can help you find and keep a happy life.

It sounds like a simple goal, doesn't it? Happiness! How many people do you know who are truly happy? How did they get that way? How can *you* find even *greater* happiness than you already have?

HOW TO READ AND UNDERSTAND
YOUR SEVEN-YEAR LIFE CYCLES

The Cosmic energy we absorb and use each day of our lives comes to us in different forms, or vibrations, which vary according to our need and stage of development.

"Every story," a creative writing professor once said to me, "has a beginning, a middle, and an end."

159

All people have the same thing. We are born, have a "middle life," and an "ending life." We pass through exact phases in our evolution on the earth. Each phase is Cosmically geared to our *need to advance* to the next phase of our Cosmic journey. Our advancement is mental, physical, and spiritual.

The stages of our evolution are easily recognized by the physical changes we undergo in the *seven-year life cycle.* There are mental and spiritual changes which coincide with these physical changes.

Let's look at the seven-year cycle for a moment. Here are the ages at which we pass from one seven-year period to another:

Age 7   14   21   28   35   42   49   56   63   70   77   84

Just looking at this arrangement is enough to spark the realization of how this cycle works. Age seven ends childhood, age 14 begins the adolescent period, age 21 starts adulthood. There are distinct physical changes represented by these seven-year periods.

The seven-year cycle also represents either a positive or a negative experience pattern. If you are in a negative cycle during any of the above periods, you find yourself the victim of fate, of "bad" luck. Everything you do seems to be wrong no matter how hard you try.

If you are in a positive cycle things seem to go your way, and you find yourself the recipient of blessings and rewarding opportunities.

HOW TO WORK WITH YOUR LIFE CYCLE

You can be happy in either a positive or negative life cycle. The metaphysical key to adjusting to your cycle in a profitable way is the Law of Life Cycles. This law states: *everything happens for a purpose, an infinite purpose.* Even the smallest, most coincidental experiences, are part of a greater Master Plan.

The students of the deeper teachings know that when they are in a negative cycle *the thing to do is hold, taking no action, or as little action as possible.* Major decisions and changes are postponed until a favorable cycle has resumed. This is exactly the opposite of the way many people operate. Often the tendency is to "fight" circumstances, all circumstances, when a negative cycle exists.

From a metaphysical viewpoint, a negative cycle is only the foundation for a positive cycle. It is the "storm" before the calm. So our objective as Cosmosis practitioners is to live through the negative cycles with as little conflict and difficulty as possible. Then, when the positive cycle is with us, we can take advantage of every opportunity to decide, take action, *soar* in a really *big* way. We practice all of the Cosmosis techniques, methods, and suggestions—no matter what the cycle brings to us.

How Tina Used Her Negative Cycle to Build a Fortune

Tina L. was in a negative cycle and she knew it. Her husband had passed on, leaving only a small insurance policy. Her children had grown and married and she lived in the lower portion of a two-family dwelling which she owned. Her health wasn't good and she was faced with first one negative condition and then another. Her car broke down on her vacation, her furnace broke down in the middle of winter, and the city insisted on taking part of her side yard as a right-of-way for a new gas main.

There were the little things too, the petty annoyances and daily inconveniences.

Tina knew through Cosmosis that this was a time to "wait and see." She wasn't going to make major decisions.

161

When she received the money from her late husband's insurance policy, it was time to use her knowledge of Cosmosis guidance. She invested it in another small two-family home. She sold it and purchased a four-family apartment building. She sold the four-family building and purchased a ten-unit building. Other properties followed.

Today, Tina has a small fortune in real estate. Her net worth has increased from several thousand dollars to several hundred thousand.

How Mike Used a Positive Cycle to Expand His Business

Mike owned several automatic laundry installations. When he became a student of Cosmosis, he was in a negative cycle. He was holding his own, paying his bills, and making a slight profit after living expenses. But, he was not doing as well as he had hoped. He also sensed intuitively that things would be better soon.

Mike's life cycles seemed to peak in the middle and were low as he approached the next cycle. He was 35 when he started his Cosmosis training—a low period for him. We expected that he'd hit his high midway between 35 and 42, so we wanted to develop a "goal-oriented" life that would help Mike reach a zenith of productivity and happiness during his positive cycle.

We started with Mike, as he was, with what he had. Mike was *planning* during his negative cycle for the success he would have during his next positive phase. He adopted the following plan for being goal-oriented, and when he came into his positive period, he capitalized on his Cosmosis training and gained more wealth, influence, and personal satisfaction than he'd ever had in his entire life up to that point. His wife was delighted with the new status that his success made possible. They bought a new home, were better able to educate their children, and even took a month's vacation in Europe—something that had always been a dream.

HOW TO PLAN A GOAL ORIENTATION PROGRAM THAT PAYS BIG DIVIDENDS

Here is how you can plan during your negative cycles to take advantage of the positive forces that will be coming your way when you are in the next positive cycle:

1. *Decide What Your Immediate, Intermediate, and Long-Range Goals Are.* What do you want to do this year? The next three to five years? The next five to ten years?

2. *Before You Take Any Major Steps in the Present, Ask Yourself How These Steps Will Affect Your Ability to Reach Your Intermediate and Long-Range Goals*. If your action deters those goals, then do not proceed with it.

3. *Determine in Advance the Methods You Will Use to Evaluate Your Progress as You Move Toward Your Goals.* Make sure that your goals are attainable.

4. *When You Are Blocked or Frustrated in Your Attempt to Reach your Goals, Find Ways to Circumvent these Negations Through Your Practice of Cosmosis.*

5. *Be Sure to Spend the Major Portion of Your Energy and Time on the Attainment of Your Goals Rather Than on the Frustrations*. Although it will be necessary to remove frustrating conditions, do not spend all of your time and attention on them. Most of your effort should be directed toward the goals themselves.

6. *Initiate Action Which Will Take You to Your Goal.* Do not wait for "ideal" circumstances. Nothing is brought about in the perfect situation. Everything requires that you *do* something before "everything falls into place." Act deliberately, with safeguards, and be aware of all the risks. Do not act out of panic, emotional stress, or a desire

to "change everything all at once." If there is one major teaching to be gained from the theory of life cycles, it is that everything evolves, progresses, from one stage or state to another. The rapid, sudden changes are often deceptive, allowing disappointment and disillusionment to set in.

7. *Adjust Yourself to the Realities of the Situation.* Try not to choose impossible goals or "far out" things. It is better to be a little more conservative at first and then be pleasantly surprised later than to be disappointed all the way along. With this attitude guiding you, inventive thinking and creative action will be present. You won't rule out completely any course of action until it proves itself to you one way or the other. Be on the lookout for the new possibilities of reaching your goals.

HOW TO MAKE MINOR ADJUSTMENTS
THROUGH DREAM MATERIAL

Your dreams are doorways to the deeper levels of your consciousness. They can help you make minor adjustments in your life which can lead to greater happiness and fulfillment. If you are meditating regularly, you will be reaching greater insights about yourself which lead to self-understanding, analysis, and adjustment.

Often dreams offer a shortcut to self-understanding, because the "raw material" of your dreams arises from the subconscious. Fears, conflicts, desires, and even forbidden wishes are unearthed. Knowing what these inner impulses are and how they guide your life, directs you to adjust your actions for greater satisfaction.

This dream interpretation work can be done in either negative or positive cycles. Here is how you can do it:

1. *Keep a Dream Pad Handy Beside Your Bed.* Each morning as you awaken, record the detail of your dreams, if

any. On those days that you are not aware of having any dream, simply mark down your feelings along with any other thoughts which come to your mind.

2. *Meditate According to the Breathing Method Outlined in Chapter 1.* Do this each day or every other day to keep your Kundalini up.

3. *After You Have Meditated for Cosmosis, Slowly Go Over Your Dream Pad and Ask Yourself What Each Dream Symbolizes.* What is the deeper meaning to you? What does it tell you about your inner motivation and need as a person? What can you learn about personal relationships?

Mike, mentioned earlier in this chapter, used this dream interpretation method to better understand his wife and to develop a closer love relationship. The natural by-product of a happy marriage was increased efficiency in his business and financial life. He understood himself more thoroughly and was able to work his way around his shortcomings. For Mike it was a Cosmosis "plus" that he hadn't counted on.

HOW TO OVERCOME KARMIC CONDITIONS FROM PAST LIVES

Progress from one life to another is measured by our ability to demonstrate love, harmony, and attunement with the God-Force and be instruments of Cosmosis. *As we are guided, protected, and led by the divinity within, we grow and develop into higher states of consciousness. To the extent that we spread hatred, disharmony, and lack of alignment with the God-Force, we are held back in our progress into the light of higher consciousness.*

When we fail to take advantage of the Cosmic opportunities to live in accordance with the laws of peace toward all things, we come back to the earth plane to lead another

165

life. Reincarnation occurs so that we can make the Cosmic lessons part of divine awareness.

We bring along with us into the world not only the inhibiting factors from previous lives but also the talents and abilities, the lessons learned, which can help us in our advancement in this life.

If we have misused our divinity in previous lives we have Karmic indebtedness to overcome before we can progress into a higher form of life or into a more Cosmically harmonious and creative life.

Karmic debts are overcome as we spread the light of our full potential as spiritual beings.

The "sticky points" of life, our tendency to repeat the same self-damaging actions, are caused by Karmic debts which must be overcome.

The fast and easy way to overcome all previous Karma is to devote oneself totally to helping others by being a complete Cosmic instrument. This kind of person, rare in our society, is guided not by his own needs but by the greater dictates of Cosmic consciousness. In mystical traditions, this is referred to as "Walking in the Christ Light" or "Living According to the Ways of the I AM I." It is a selfless existence—an egoless way of life.

This kind of life is difficult for most of us to follow. But there are ways of approximating a life-style which has a small amount of "self" and a high degree of "Cosmosis."

Although it may seem, at first, that less concern for yourself might lead to less happiness, quite the opposite is the case. The happiest people are those dedicated to something or someone, to some project or faith, which is more important than their own welfare. Scientists, artists, writers, musicians, the great people of all ages, are directed by an inner urge to create, to understand, to relate.

You can be your own creative personality, a philosopher in your own way.

One of the most dedicated groups of people I've ever

met was at Bell Telephone Laboratories in New Jersey. There America's greatest concentration of brainpower is paid to *think* about the way things are and about the way they could be. Some of them become so absorbed in the majesty of discovery that they forget to eat a meal or go home at night. They live not for themselves alone but for the lure of the unknown—the transistor, the laser beam, space exploration, undersea navigation, advanced communication.

I once witnessed a rehearsal of the Pittsburgh Symphony Orchestra. There, a group of people dedicated to the joys of music were putting aside self-concerns to elevate the human spirit and express man's highest aspiration. You see how this kind of devotion can be yours, too. Life can be lived for more than personal comfort alone. It can be lived for spiritual awareness.

Let's see what you can do to become Cosmically attuned and dedicated to the things, ideas, and activities that have transcendental significance.

1. *Introduce Yourself to the World of Art and Music.* Here's a real chance to get away from yourself and make contact with the greatest minds of all time. Don't just listen to music as a time-filler. Study art. Get personally involved in music. Study its deeper meaning, the keys it has for your own self-liberation

2. *Read the Great Books.* If you feel at home with ideas expressed in words, you might like to take on a hobby of reading the classics. Poetry might appeal to you. A good beginning is just to make sure you read the books on the best-seller lists.

3. *Become Familiar with Current Events.* Maybe you'll find it easier to understand contemporary art, music, and literature. Possibly the world of science appeals more. Politics, religion, fashion, and the entertainment world all can be found in magazines and on television. Know what is going on, what the trends are, and what the future is likely to

hold. Escape from yourself and rub shoulders, through knowledge, with the most creative minds of our time. It is easy to do. It is inexpensive to buy a current events magazine. A few moments each week planning your television viewing can take you literally around the world in search of the new, unusual, and stimulating.

4. *Choose Your Friends.* The old saying is that "birds of a feather flock together." Choose to be with people who are *thinking and doing.* Forget the phoney people who are out to impress, dominate, or take advantage of you. Be with the creative, loving, outgoing, selfless people.

5. *Avoid "Sticky" Situations.* One sure way to avoid Karmic debts is to stay away from self-destructive situations. If you know that negation, hatred, jealousy, and self-interests are occurring within a group of people, at the job or on social occasions, avoid it. If you know you are bound to be emotionally "tied up" by someone, avoid that person. Once people recognize that you have absorbed psychic powers through Cosmosis, they will gravitate to you with their problems. Don't take on more than you can handle. Don't let other people—strangers or family members—drain your energy or emotional vitality. Give them love and concern. Be sure to give your constructive attention, keeping it all on a higher level. Try to elevate their thoughts and actions. As you help others to advance in the light of Cosmic consciousness, you will advance too.

How Mrs. W.W. Overcame Her Karma

Mrs. W.W. was the middle-aged wife of a corporation executive. Her adverse Karma evidenced itself in her strained relationship to her husband. She complained bitterly about his absence from her on many evenings because of business commitments. She disliked business entertaining, his long trips away from her, and what she felt was his lack of concern for the family. In other words, her attitude was "Why aren't you giving more to me?" Only rarely did she consider what she could do to make life easier and more comfortable for her husband. Quite naturally, as a result of her self-attitude, her husband spent even less time with her. He resented her nagging and complaining. After a busy day, he wanted to relax and "gear down." Instead, he was faced with more turmoil and trouble from Mrs. W.W.

All of the arguments were tearing at Mrs. W.W. The more she tried to put things into harmony, the more she was alienated from her husband.

She decided to enroll in one of our classes on Cosmosis. That was the turning point. She concluded that she should dedicate her life to others. Charity work, self-improvement reading, and music became her hobbies. Mr. W.W. found a loving, understanding, supportive wife at home. She was willing to listen to his problems and become interested in his hobbies, which were sailing and golf. She spent time with him, leisure time, and got to know him all over again. She realized that she had been living with a stranger for several years. He had advanced and changed. Her "new" husband turned out to be more loving and attentive than her old one. Why? Because she had placed "him" before her own desires and needs. Her consciousness was on others. Obviously, she had learned the Karmic lesson. She was advancing into the light of her own truth.

**How the Simpsons Found the Place
That Made Them Happy**

Happiness is not always a matter of geography or the "place" that you are. But some "places" are more suitable to your vibration and level of consciousness than others. This became evident to a couple, Mr. and Mrs. Simpson, who were following our plan to overcome their Karma. They felt as though they were in a Karmic "rut." Mr. and Mrs. Simpson wanted to get away for a while. He had

169

several weeks of vacation time. They flew from their east coast home to Florida. They rented a car to tour as much of the state as they had time for.

The object of the tour was to visit cultural centers, historic sites, and geographic "wonders." They avoided entertainment for its own sake and instead chose their travel destinations based on educational and uplifting opportunities.

The Simpsons loved Florida.

Six months later, they moved to Florida because Mr. Simpson was accepted for a job he had applied for while they were on vacation. They are happy in their new home and they've found, through Cosmosis, the way of life which suits them. They are healthy, prosperous, and are looking forward to many youthful years of dream living.

Overcoming Karmic debt inherited from past lives and increasing progress is a little different for each of us. Sometimes a small adjustment in our life-style is enough to raise our level of consciousness and purpose. When our *reason* for living includes something more than pure personal comfort, we are on the road to demonstrating the harmony and love which make restitution for the mistakes of past lives. By placing ourselves in touch with the very best thought and the highest human expression through Cosmosis, we create a psychic link to the source of man's spiritual elevation.

THE LAW OF KARMIC ATTRACTION
BUILDS YOUR FUTURE

Karma is the cause-and-effect law of the universe which states that *everything we do, say, or think affects what happens to us in the future.* When we overcome the effects of negative past actions, we are creating new, positive Karma which moves us higher in our state of evolution

You and I are building our Karma right this minute. What we are doing now will affect that which happens to us tomorrow. What we do in *this existence* will affect our *future existences* or states of consciousness.

By being concerned for the welfare of others, we build the positive Karma which places us in closer touch with the God-Power of the universe, Cosmosis.

HOW COSMIC ATTUNEMENT
MAKES YOU HAPPIER

You have a right to be happy.

You can live an exciting life, brimming with the riches and adventure that Cosmosis will manifest for you. Work to make the most of your present life cycle and build to take advantage of the next one. By building your own goal-oriented program, you can plan for the future you want, for the extra happiness which should be yours.

Work with the forces in your life, rather than against them. Anything that happens to you can be a steppingstone to greater attunement and to higher realization of your purpose in this life. Even negative experiences can set the stage for a Cosmic inundation of blessings which are beyond your wildest imagination.

There are two aspects of happiness. One is the attainment of your goals. The other is the ability not to be thrown off by disappointments. Cosmic attunement, your knowledge of how to relate to all experiences, will help you place disappointment in the right light, to use it to gain the next step in your unfoldment.

Examples of How Disappointments Led
to Greater Happiness Through Cosmosis

Mr. G.R. was dismissed from a middle-management position with an automotive supply firm; he promptly found a job that paid more and gave him more freedom to make decisions.

Mrs. F.G. was disappointed because her daughter married a foreign student while she was away at college. Today, the daughter is living in luxury in a foreign country where her husband is a high government official. She is the mother of three children and is able to visit her mother twice a year. It was because Mrs. F.G. accepted the Cosmic working out of this ideal marriage that she was able to share in the blessings and joy which her daughter is experiencing.

Mr. D.K. was disappointed because of his marriage which ended in divorce and bitterness. He had planned for years of happiness and his hopes were dashed by the breakup. But he accepted the disappointment and invoked the power of Cosmosis. His small plumbing business has increased tenfold, and he is on the verge of marrying his lovely secretary. Happiness is his. He is building his goal-orientation program and is uplifting his thoughts with cultural activities to help overcome negative Karma.

Miss R.R. was a fashion photographer with a booming promotional agency. She was taken off a key account and placed on assignment to several new, small companies. It looked as though she had been demoted.

But Miss R.R. accepted the new assignment, knowing that Cosmosis would make it a steppingstone to something else. Within six months, one of the small accounts she was working with became very large and she worked on it exclusively. She received a raise and her work on this was more fulfilling and creative than any she had ever done! A disappointment had led to greater happiness.

POINTS TO REMEMBER FROM THIS CHAPTER

1. There are mental, physical, and spiritual changes that we undergo in life which help us to advance. These changes are represented by seven-year life cycles. Negative cycles are foundations for positive cycles.

2. A goal orientation program can help you prepare to take advantage of upcoming positive cycles with Cosmosis.

3. Dream material can give you personal insight that will help you to make the minor adjustments you need to be happier in life.

4. By overcoming the negative effects of previous lives, working out Karmic patterns, you are lifted to a higher state of consciousness through association with man's best expression in art, music, literature, and current events.

5. Working with the Cosmic forces in your life, including the disappointments, will help build a foundation for greater happiness.

Chapter 11

HOW TO CALL AN ASCENDED MASTER OR GURU FOR PSYCHIC HELP

You have a spiritual teacher and personal guardian.

You may not yet know who your master teacher is or how you can be helped by him. This chapter will show you *how* to make contact with *your* master, how to get *exact answers* to your questions through your master, and how to make contact with *other entities and energies in the spirit world.*

The modern science of spiritual contact and communication with the other side of life has been taking place since the middle of the nineteenth century. We know that the spiritual world intersects and participates in our physical world. We've also found out that the spiritual world consists of energies and entities, each of which is separate and distinct. Some are personalities which contain a conscious element similar to our own. They talk and think and behave in a very human way. Yet, since they are pure spirit they are able to make attunement with Cosmosis easily, making their work on the earth plane seem superhuman.

THE PLANES OF SPIRITUAL EXISTENCE

There are several planes or levels of spiritual awareness that you are likely to contact.

1. *The Astral Plane.* The first level seems to be inhabited by spirit entities that have recently left the earth. They "reside" on this level until they are able to advance to a higher plane. Some seem to leave this plane quickly to reincarnate on earth again. They do not advance until their Karma is complete. Some, called "earth-bound spirits," hover between earth life and the afterlife of the astral plane. These lower-level entities are usually responsible for hauntings and poltergeist activity (the movement of objects). Earth-bound spirits are easy to contact. However, without the proper training in discernment, a student can make contact with those earth-bound spirits who are spiritual parasites, sapping energy from the living. Often uncontrolled trance work manifests itself and the entity tries to take over the life of the student. Protection is available for this type of condition. It is possible to ward off and drive out such malicious spirits.

2. *The Ascended Plane.* This more refined level seems to contain the more highly evolved and beneficial spirits. Here the master teachers of all ages attempt to lift mankind into harmonious alignment with the God-Force that leads to eventual union with Pure Divinity. This is the level of contact that this chapter will teach you to make. The ascended plane channels energy, direction, and guidance to all who are sincere in their seeking.

3. *The Cosmic or God Plane.* The level of *Cosmic consciousness* is the force behind the force, the cause of the universe itself. This is the God-level of pure energy, pure spirit, Infinite Intelligence, the I AM I. All spirits eventually reunite with this God Center. The purpose of all existence is to find unification with this Transcendental Reality.

176

HOW COSMOSIS SETS UP
THE PROPER WAVELENGTH
FOR SPIRIT CONTACT

Let's go back to our original definition for a moment. What is Cosmosis? It is the energy, the universal spiritual component in everything. It manifests in different forms. We use these various forms, or frequencies, to create psychic phenomena for dynamic living. By tapping in on Cosmosis and reforming or focusing it, we activate the extrasensory capacities of the superconscious mind. Contact with the higher realms of existence is only one of many forms of extrasensory ability.

THE MASTER KEY FOR CONTACTING
YOUR PERSONAL GUIDE

The master key, according to Raja Yoga, for awakening the latent extrasensory ability—and hence power to contact a master teacher—is meditation.

There are, as we've seen in this book, many forms of meditation. There is one which is excellent for meeting your ascended master teacher, guru, or personal guide.

It isn't possible to coerce the spirits. But we can make ourselves as receptive to contact as possible. We can do those things which make it possible for the spirit world to reach us easily.

Group meditation, carefully controlled and encouraged, attracts the very highest spirit messengers from the ascended plane. These masters are able to:

* Guide you in making decisions.
* Channel healing, love, and protection to you.
* Multiply your ability to control your future destiny.
* Warn you of impending dangers.

177

* Notify you if someone is about to take advantage of you.
* Present the wisdom of the ages and Cosmic secrets.
* Help you to attract wealth, success, and recognition.
* Increase your psychic ability for mental telepathy.
* Help you to travel astrally when you sleep.
* Bring messages from your loved ones and friends who have passed on.
* Direct other spirit messengers and Cosmic energies to assist you in all aspects of your life.

A SEANCE MEDITATION FOR CONTACT
WITH THE ASCENDED MASTERS

Group work for contact with individual masters is a little more elaborate than the group work for amplification of occult power, but the Cosmosis method is similar. The first step is complete and absolute dedication to the spirit world. Decide that you will allow your master to help in every phase of your life. Your mental, emotional, physical, and spiritual welfare will be the constant concern of your master if you have faith in his presence, and *if you are willing to follow his promptings.* The basic steps are as follows:

1. Gather together a like-minded group of friends *for an evening meeting* to make contact. Make certain that your friends are as dedicated to making contact with their masters as you are. All other reasons for holding a seance should be put aside. The single purpose of this group meditation should be uppermost in everyone's mind.

2. At the appointed time, gather together in the darkness

and play some recorded music, or sing, or let one of the members play live music to raise the Cosmosis vibration.

3. At the conclusion of the music, direct a prayer-statement to the spirits asking that the masters may make themselves known to the assembled sitters. You might like to use something like: "Infinite Intelligence, we ask that our spirit loved ones, messengers, and friends may be with us this evening to help us reach the ascended master teachers of all ages. We are sitting to receive word from our personal guides. We are turning our lives over to them for direction and help. May their presences be with each of us here tonight."

4. Sit in absolute silence for at least half an hour.

5. Encourage the sitters to describe the impressions that they are getting, or have gotten, in detail.

6. As the sitters share their impressions and messages from the spirit, try to interpret the meaning of the symbols, visions, and voices that are described. Ascended master dictations are not always literal or completely clear at first—unless you have a trance medium in the group—but they do come together like parts of a puzzle or links in a chain.

7. Maintain the meditational mood and the free, spontaneous sharing and interpreting of the impressions. Once the identity of individual masters is established, you will find that the messages and impressions demonstrate specific information for each sitter.

8. After a number of sessions have been held to make contact with the masters, it is possible for the sitters to disband or meet only occasionally. From this point on, each sitter may make contact with his or her master while sitting alone in silent meditation.

9. Regular contact through silent meditation is essential. Masters are like people in that they lose interest if they are ignored.

179

10. When a problem or decision arises, contact with the master should be made before action is taken.

Let's see how this Cosmosis-inspired meditational method has worked for the members of one of our study groups.

Typical Ascended Master Contacts and Their Results

Ethel J. had a small antique shop. Business was not good. Her master was a monk from the Far East. She could see him in her mind's eye and she carried on lengthy conversations with him during meditation. He advised her to move the location of her shop. He even gave her an approximate location where there was space available. She drove to the recommended spot and there was a shop for rent. She moved her entire stock of merchandise and within a year her business had doubled.

Bob L. was trying to find himself. After years of "searching" for the meaning of life which included several jobs, two wives, and a bout with poor health, his master led him into the realm of spirit in such a way as to change his entire outlook. He found that his mission in life was to serve, not just to take or demand. He learned how to give, to love, and be a Cosmic instrument. His master was an ancient Egyptian teacher of the mysteries. He slowly went over Bob's life, a step at a time, and showed him how he made mistakes, what he had to do to overcome them.

Maria R. had soul flights or astral trips during her sleep which were led by her master. The secrets of the Cosmos were revealed to her. Maria became one of the finest psychic practitioners that I know of as a result of this hidden wisdom which was revealed. She was "elected" to receive protection, guidance, and a sense of security and peace of mind which only a rare few obtain. Now she is helping others to find their masters and she is using Cosmosis methods in a development class which she teaches.

Talbert T. was suffering from acute abdominal attacks. He joined a group to reach his master in order to ask for healing help. He had been in and out of the hospital several times. Little or no improvement was present, and he had to take strong sedatives in order to live with the discomfort.

Talbert's master turned out to be a European nun from the 15th century who was gifted with healing power. She worked with him each day during his meditation. Talbert could feel the warmth of the penetrating spiritual rays which she directed into his body. A cure was fast and thorough. The doctors were amazed and delighted. To them, the affliction had disappeared as mysteriously as it had appeared.

This nun stayed with Talbert and assisted him in his business decisions. She warned him when he was about to make the wrong move and urged him on when he was on the right course. His intuitive sense improved until he displayed amazing mental telepathy. He was able to read the intentions of others, both friends and foes alike. He used Cosmosis techniques to expand his control and domination of the actions of others as well. In fact, he was led to adopt Cosmosis because his master directed him to apply the advanced techniques in his life.

MAKING DECISIONS
WITH YOUR MASTER'S HELP

If you are in regular contact with your master, you will be able to carry on complete conversations in your mind's ear, as it were. During quiet times alone with your master, you will have the opportunity to ask for advice on little matters as well as on *big* decisions.

The reason decision making is so important is that once we decide something, we then usually act on the decision. These actions set up a Cosmic series of reactions, cause and effect situations. These "unknown" situations, coming toward us in time, can profoundly affect the kind of future we will attract.

Remember that your master is helping the total you, the you that is hidden from others, the you that has faults, strengths, and desires. He is reconciling your spiritual self with the mental and physical self. He knows your past, the present, and your future. In other words, he has all the facts. You have only a portion of the insight that he has. So there will be times that his spiritual advice may seem strange, contradictory, or even misleading. But it is not. There may be a situation of which he is cognizant which you do not yet comprehend.

Your master will not help you unless you follow all directions exactly—no matter how contradictory they may seem at the time. It would not pay to get an attorney's advice and then refuse to take it. It would be equally unwise to see a doctor and then ignore his help.

If you ignore the directions of the spirit too often, you will be deserted.

Sit in silent meditation and "bring in" your master by making mental contact with him. Present your questions and wait for his reply. The impressions that you get should be noted down if they are symbolic so that you can get the additional parts to the "puzzle" as you sit again. Your master may bring your spirit loved ones and friends to you so that they can also comment on the problem which you are trying to solve.

Your own, personal master is also able to focus other spiritual energies for your use in manifesting better health, more youth and vitality, and greater psychic powers.

How Clyde Was Saved
from a Robbery by His Master

Clyde S. lived in a large city where the crime rate was high. He had a small loan and check cashing business on a heavily traveled street. Each evening he was escorted by the police to the bank to make his deposit. He had followed the same procedure for many years. As his assistant was locking up, he was preparing the deposit, counting the money, and making last-minute notations. He would then call the police and tell them that he was ready to go to the bank.

Clyde was a student of Cosmosis and during one of his meditations with his master, he received a distinct warning about the evening "lockup routine." The message he got was not to let all of the customers in. This didn't make too much sense at the time, but it did later that same evening.

As Clyde was preparing his deposit in his office, he heard his assistant talking to someone outside the main door. "I'm sorry, we are closing now," he said.

The door had already been locked and a man wanted to be let in at the last minute. Clyde thought of his master's message and sensed danger. He left his office to see what was happening. His assistant was about to unlock the door and let the customer in when Clyde motioned to him *not* to open the door. He called his assistant away from the front of the building.

That did it! The man at the door quickly moved away. Clyde felt a sense of relief.

The next morning he heard the news. A robbery had been committed at the all-night drugstore next to his loan company. The man who owned the store was wounded and the robber was shot to death as he was leaving with the money.

The man who was shot was the same one who had tried to enter Clyde's loan company at closing time.

Was Clyde the intended robbery victim? The spirit had warned him and by following the message he was spared.

How Joyce Received Messages from Her Relatives

Joyce L. found her master who had been a medical doctor near Boston at the turn of the century. He was a student of history and geography as well as a physician and surgeon. Joyce was also interested in these subjects and they had many a fascinating discussion together. Usually they talked about the books which Joyce was reading.

Then one day her master, Doctor Peterson, announced that "others" were "here" to talk to Joyce. First her mother came in, then her grandfather, and a boy who had been killed in an automobile accident near her home the previous summer. At first Joyce wondered if her imagination or subconscious mind was manufacturing these conversations. She enjoyed frequent visits from these three. They talked of many things, their lives, the future, and Joyce's everyday activities.

Finally, the boy who was in the automobile accident asked Joyce to relay a message to his mother who lived just a few blocks away from Joyce. If the mother recognized the message as valid, then Joyce could be *assured* that she was not imagining things.

The message referred to some photographs of the boy which his mother was keeping. The boy requested that the photograph of him and his grandfather, who was also in spirit, be given to his grandmother who was still living on earth. It was a specific message. Joyce knew nothing about the photograph herself, so she could not have "invented" the message.

184

Joyce called the boy's mother and told her what she had received. The mother was delighted to get the message from her son. She knew exactly which photograph was referred to and did give it to her mother as a special gift. Everyone was pleased and thankful that Joyce had been given this little word of love and concern from the other side.

More messages came through Joyce with the help of her master. Often people who want to contact someone on the other side will write to Joyce and ask her to see if she can make contact. With the help of her master, she is helping many people communicate from one plane to another.

It is a blessing to be able to do such wonderful work and it is all because of a medical doctor named Peterson who is interested in history and geography.

How Sally's Career as a Sculptor Was Guided by Spirit

Sally taught art history at a junior college. She was proficient at sculpting and had the deep inner feeling that she was about to start a new phase of her work. She was using Cosmosis to help her organize her life to get the most she could in terms of satisfaction and happiness.

Sally was in a development group that was seeking contact with the spirit world. Sally received an American Indian as a guide. Red Horse was his name, and he was a big, humorous man who took an interest in her artistic work.

He brought inspiration and guidance while Sally was working. His presence gave her a fresh point of view and a new perspective in her work. Red Horse joked and laughed with her and gave her a light touch and a more bouyant attitude toward her work. No longer did she take herself so seriously. She was able to "let go" and relax and ask for the spiritual help which she needed to really dig in and do beautiful work.

Sally became one of the most talented artists in her school and developed national recognition and a reputation for being an emerging force in the art world.

She gives the credit to Red Horse who taught her to laugh and to be playful with her work. Now she enjoys everything she does because she has had the success and recognition that she needed to spur her on to even more challenging creations.

HOW TO USE YOUR MASTER
TO HELP YOUR FRIENDS

Your master can help your friends. Just communicate a need which a friend has and your master will intercede to help with healing, to find a solution to a difficulty, or to lead the way into more favorable conditions.

When you are sitting in meditation with your master, let him know what the problem is or who he should go and help. You may find out that your friend was visited at the very time you asked your master to intercede.

Mr. S.S. directed his master to aid his mother who was in the hospital for a serious operation. She actually felt and saw the master while she was under anesthesia on the operating table. He brought many psychic surgeons from the spirit world who helped the earth doctors perform open heart surgery.

Miss P.L. asked her master to watch over her fiancee while he was serving in the armed forces overseas. After his tour of active duty, he returned safely and married Miss P.L. His letters often contained references to an "invisible" spiritual protection which was with him all of the time. He had several narrow escapes when he was in a combat zone which he attributes to his "shield of protection." He remarked, "I was destined to return. It was in the cards for me. Someone has been looking out for me."

Mr. S.Q. changed his investment portfolio because his master directed him to change from holdings in blue chip companies to smaller, more growth-oriented firms. Within a year's time his net worth increased rapidly, and now he does almost all of his investing after he has talked with his master. Mr. S.Q. realizes, too, that he is "being given wealth for a greater Cosmic purpose which will be revealed." He is on the right track with respect to his money consciousness so he can't make wrong decisions.

Mrs. J.R. asked her master to help her son who was arrested on a narcotics charge. He was placed on probation and his life changed for the better. He is attending school to learn computer programming and intends to get married. His contacts with the world of drugs are entirely shut off, they are a thing of the past, and he looks forward to a happy and normal future.

HOW TO PROTECT YOURSELF
FROM LOWER ASTRAL ENTITIES

Evil and malicious entities can come through to you and influence your thought-forms and even your mental and physical health. This is likely to happen if your motives for contacting spirits are low. If you are wishing destruction, pain, failure, or mental anguish on anyone, you are likely to find yourself in league with the *dark forces.*

Protection from psychic attack by lower astral entities and earth-bound spirits will be guaranteed if you:

* Make contact with spirits for the *betterment* of self, but not for purely selfish reasons.

187

* Ask through prayer, meditation, and affirmation to be placed in touch with the higher levels of spirit.

* Test your motives when you submit a request or petition to a spirit.

* Make sure that you are willing to be a Cosmic instrument, not a manipulator and exploiter of the laws of the universe.

* Work with your master primarily. Avoid contact with less familiar spirits.

* When you visit a seance with strangers present, be cautious and examine the manifestations critically.

* Try not to discuss your spiritual blessings too openly. Speak with trusted friends and others with a similar viewpoint.

CONTACTING ILLUMINATED SOULS ON THE EARTH PLANE

You may be lucky enough to find a master who is living on the earth plane. Living masters are highly evolved souls who have made contact with the higher levels of spirit and are guided and directed by the inner glow of this alignment. They channel prophetic and vitally significant messages from the higher planes or from a spiritual hierarchy.

Your life may be drastically changed by contact with a soul of light, an illuminated living master.

Spirit directs these meetings with living masters. You may also come in contact with temporarily illuminated beings who are in your life to place a realization or blessing at your doorstep. Do not be surprised at such a meeting or experience. You will meet such a person when you are ready. It is not necessary to search for a living master teacher. You will be found by him.

Those who are temporarily illuminated may be pure spiritual instruments on one occasion and rather mundane and ordinary at other times. But they have their mission to fulfill just as well. And you may be lucky enough to share in their understanding. Since you are a student of Cosmosis, the likelihood of your meeting such an illuminated one is above average.

Cosmosis is the energy of illumination. You might also become a pure spiritual instrument. All that you do may be guided by the higher forces, and you might undertake a mission of helping others on the earth plane. You may advance much more than you think. A step toward mastery of Cosmosis and even a little knowledge of the vast power of the Cosmic laws and their operation is enough to start the ball rolling. Cosmosis does the rest. All you have to do is ride the crest of the gentle power which is shaping your life, at this very instant, for the better.

You have been taken this far.

You have the infinite storehouse of spiritual treasures at your fingertips. Cosmosis will be with you always to assist, to guard, to renew and regenerate your life.

Let's move on and see, in the following chapter, how Cosmosis can bring out your hidden talents.

Points to Remember from This Chapter

1. Spirit beings reside in one of several levels of consciousness called planes of existence. They are the astral plane, the ascended plane, and the Cosmic or God plane. Cosmosis sets up the proper wavelength for contact with these planes. Group meditation and seance work "brings in" your master. After he has been identified, you may work with him alone.

2. Your master helps to summon other entities and energies. Since your master is pure spirit, he is able to help when he is called upon. Decisions made

189

with your master's help will work for your benefit. Your master can even help your friends.

3. As long as your intentions are good, you will not contact lower astral entities and earth-bound spirits. As a student of Cosmosis, you are likely to meet a living master during your lifetime.

Chapter 12

HOW COSMOSIS
BRINGS OUT TALENT YOU NEED

We've come a long way in this book, you and I, along the pathway of self-understanding through Cosmosis. We've seen how the creative force of the universe is working all of the time. We have but to place ourselves in attunement with it, and its manifesting laws, to shape the way of life which brings us everything we want and need.

Now we are ready to energize your talents and hidden abilities with Cosmosis.

You are now in a position to be inventive with *every-thing* you do. *You* can now amaze people with *your* new ideas. *You can tap the deep riches of your own potential.*

You can be creative—all of the time—with Cosmosis.

WHAT CREATIVITY IS
AND HOW COSMOSIS INCREASES IT

Creativity is the ability to bring something into being for the first time. If you are a creator, you are an originator, an innovator, a self-motivator. Your imagination is the cause-force of your creativity. Thus, conformity and duplication are the antitheses of creation. If you try to "fit into a mold" created by someone else, your way of life will make creative thinking and freedom of action very difficult. *Cosmosis, the life energy of the universe, releases the shackles of artificially imposed thinking and preplanned behavior.* Cosmosis opens up infinite combinations, multiple possibilities, for your consideration and use. Cosmosis puts you in touch with the source of originality and creativity, God.

In the most profound way, creativity is God expressing through you. This does not mean you must be religious to be creative. In fact, you do not have to "have faith" in God to be creative. But, you *must* "be yourself."

Being yourself, allowing your full, inner person to create, to *express,* means that the Highest Force, God, is manifesting in you.

You have hidden talent now which can be brought out when you allow the best in you to manifest itself.

How Peter Broke with Preplanned Behavior and Became Creative

The most stifling kind of thinking is that which is imposed by others. When you adopt another person's values or expectations of your behavior, you are blocking Cosmosis creativity. Peter V. realized this and started early in life to hammer out his own values and his own behavior patterns.

Peter made his living as a chemical engineer. But his hobby was organic gardening. He and his wife spent many hours raising prize-winning flowers, fruits, and vegetables. After several years of doing work for a large chemical company, he decided to abandon preplanned behavior. He was not going to continue his work at the chemical company, although his position guaranteed him a very comfortable and lucrative life until retirement. His friends thought he was crazy to leave his job.

Instead, Peter decided to look for work that would allow him to be more creative—to think, to test, to discover. His wife was in agreement with him, so he sent out resumés to search for another job.

Peter found just the right position doing basic research at an agricultural college. He was able to combine his chemical training with his acquired knowledge of organic farming.

How Gwen Overcame Artificial Thinking and Discovered Wealth

Gwen T. learned how to become creative with money. She did it by being unconventional and throwing off the conservative thinking she had been taught by her family.

When Gwen's father died, he left her a considerable estate. She was young and single and inclined to know talented people. A boyfriend of hers suggested that she hear a new, local singing group which was appearing at a small nightclub.

Gwen heard the group and was convinced that they had enormous potential and could go places in the entertainment business. Her boyfriend told her that the group was looking for a manager and he was thinking of putting them under contract. Although he did not know much about the business, he hoped to be able to handle their affairs in his spare time. But he told her that they needed several thousand dollars to get themselves in shape for some more important bookings.

Gwen began tuning in on the group during meditation in Cosmosis.

Gwen was directed to offer to back the group with the necessary funds if she could be a partner in managing. Her boyfriend agreed. Gwen invested several thousand dollars in the singing group and today has earned three times that as her share of the management fee.

She is going on to back other groups and manage other kinds of entertainment talent.

Gwen seems to have found the pot of gold at the end of the rainbow. She has an uncanny way of spotting potential, bringing it out, and making money with it. She is a creative person in an unconventional business, who is earning money faster than she knows what to do with it. Had she followed her early training, she never would have even considered such investments in time and money. But they are paying off handsomely for her.

The first Cosmosis rule to follow to bring out the talent you already have is: *Don't be limited to thinking imposed by family and friends, and don't plan your behavior according to someone else's values, attitudes, or expectations.*

HOW TO TAP THE DEEPER RICHES
OF YOUR OWN POTENTIAL

No matter what your stage in life is at the present, you've got potential that you don't even realize. Yes, that's right, you've got possibilities beyond your hopes and dreams. There is very little that is actually beyond your reach. With thoughtful planning and determined execution of your plans, you can tap the deeper riches of your own potential. Cosmosis can help you do it easily and completely.

Let's review a basic Cosmosis principle for a moment and see how effortlessly this can be done. Remember in earlier chapters that we pointed out how your subconscious mind contains a blueprint of everything that is going to happen to you? We showed how you can change that blueprint and in so doing change your future. This is because Cosmosis unifies all levels of mind and creates a clear channel from your conscious mind to your subcon-

194

scious, superconscious, and divine-conscious. When you are a clear channel, your conscious world is influenced by these higher mental levels.

The second Cosmosis rule to follow to bring out talent you already have is: *Clear all levels of mind and let your imagination and phantasy world run unhampered.*

You'll never know you've got talent until you find it.

Your imagination and Cosmosis energy can show you your potential. Here's how:

1. Sit in silence, relax, and let your mind work at random. See yourself doing, being, or having whatever you like. Visualize many kinds of talent and picture yourself expressing this talent—*whatever* it may be.

2. Don't limit your visualization by what you know you can do. The sky is the limit! Picture yourself doing things that you'd never have even dreamed of doing. Don't censor anything, no matter how absurd it may seem. You can do anything. You can be anything. Let yourself go!

3. Now go back over your visualizations and consider each one carefully. What reasonable, feasible possibilities suggest themselves to you as a result of your visualizations? Chances are good that one of your unhampered visualizations may prompt a course of action that is actually possible. Think in terms of what is appealing to you. Ignore practicality for the time being.

4. Choose a course of action and plan what you can do to bring your visualization into being. Don't execute your plan right away. Do plan either in your mind or on paper the step you should deliberately take.

5. If, after further consideration, you are still deeply moved to make your dream come true, start to carry out your plan.

Remember that all great discoveries were dreams at first. Most of our talented and inventive personalities have endless imaginations. When we consider the impossible, the possible shows itself to us! Your imagination is one of the greatest mental assets you have. With your imagination you can build, tear down, and build again. You can literally reorganize your life—change it with your imagination and inventiveness.

HOW TO BE INVENTIVE
WITH EVERYTHING YOU DO

What are you doing now, this week? What do you plan to do next month or a year from now? Ask yourself these questions:

* Is there a new way that I can do it?
* How about changing the order of what I'm doing?
* Is it possible to add or take away an element?
* Can I do it with someone else or in a different place?
* Have I found the most rewarding way to do it?
* Can I combine this activity with another?
* Is there a novel twist I can add to it?

Cosmosis will help you reach into the infinite for more possibilities and better ways than pure human reasoning and prudence to be inventive with everything you plan to do. By stimulating your thoughts and actions with Cosmosis energy, you'll open the doors to *greater awareness*—the secret of all worthwhile accomplishment.

The third Cosmosis rule to follow to bring out talent you already have is: *Look for novel, unusual, or unique ways to do what you are doing now.*

How Bill Found a Better Way
to Stop Smoking

Bill R. had tried several commercial ways of stopping

196

his use of cigarettes. None had worked very well. He had such a craving for his two-packs-a-day that he was miserable when he stopped. He tried chewing gum, candy, and "cigarette substitutes."

Bill knew that there had to be a better way to stop. He let his imagination run rampant with the idea. What would force him to stop? What would encourage him to stop? What would reward him if he did? Then he hit it or it hit him, through Cosmosis—a reward and punishment plan. Bill was fond of playing poker. Being cautious by nature and a lucky man at cards, he budgeted a small amount of his monthly income to the game. He never spent more than his allotted amount so he never lost more than he could afford to lose, and often he was ahead a great deal.

Bill made a deal with himself. For every pack of cigarettes he didn't smoke, he set aside double the price of those two packs for his "gambling kitty." For every pack he did smoke, he took twice the cost of that package away from his gambling money.

That cured Bill very fast. A good poker game, or any other card game for that matter, was his way of relaxing and restoring his energy. When he smoked, he was punished by not being able to gamble as much. When he didn't smoke, he was rewarded by having more money to play with. Within a week, Bill had stopped smoking entirely. After months, he's decided that he is now a confirmed nonsmoker.

How Roberta Found a Better Way to Decorate Her Apartment

Roberta D., a career woman who worked for a travel agency, loved to change the decor in her apartment every year. She insisted on designing the changes herself but she had little time to investigate possible fabrics, paint colors, furniture styles, and so forth. This made the job twice as time-consuming and difficult as it should have been. She'd run from one store to another, trying to match wallpaper, rugs, carpeting, and furniture.

She let her imagination run rampant with the idea that "there must be a better way." Then it hit her. Why not ask the suppliers of furniture, fabrics, carpets, and so forth to send their catalogues to her directly? Off went several dozen letters to manufacturers, stores, and dealers. Back came catalogues, brochures, and descriptive information. Roberta had more possibilities at her fingertips by mail than she would have had if she'd shopped in person for several years. It was the perfect answer. And it was simple to do, once she got the answer through her practice of Cosmosis.

At this writing, Roberta has decorated her apartment three times by using the catalogue material. She decides at home and then goes out and buys. She knows exactly what she wants in advance and avoids the confusion of trying to make up her mind when she is in a store.

**How Hank Found a Better Way
to Take a Vacation**

Hank V. was drawn to the fascination of travel. His wife and three daughters looked forward to his yearly vacation so they could visit a new section of the country.

One day he saw an advertisement in a magazine to enter a contest. All he had to do was write a winning last line to a verse. The first prize was an all-expense paid trip to Hawaii for two!

Other prizes were trips to other famous locations. Hank started the rituals described in Chapter 2 of this book. He knew this was a novel way to plan for a vacation, but he had absolute and complete confidence in Cosmosis pointing out the answer.

Exactly six weeks later he got the news. He had won the trip, all expenses paid, to Hawaii. With a small amount of money, his usual vacation amount, he was able to take his daughters. This was a beautiful vacation in a luxury hotel on the beach. Sight-seeing, delicious food, and heavenly weather completed this once-in-a-lifetime trip. It would have been impossible without this streak of good luck brought on by Cosmosis and Hank's willingness to look for the novel and unusual way of doing what he was already thinking about.

HOW TO DEVELOP NEW IDEAS
THAT PAY OFF

New ideas are a "dime a dozen." But ideas that pay off, that bring the kind of response which showers the originator with recognition and wealth, don't happen by accident. The Infinite Creative Power of the Universe is behind these million-dollar ideas. This Cosmosis manifestation is easier to demonstrate than most people think.

You may have had an idea recently yourself, but you pushed it aside as not practical, or too expensive, or too technical for you to perfect.

That's negative thinking. With Cosmosis helping you, you can amaze your friends, find devoted admirers, and win the applause and praise you deserve *with ideas that pay!*

The fourth Cosmosis rule to follow to bring out talent you already have is: *Before presenting a new idea, prepare people for it.*

An idea is no good unless someone buys it, accepts it, or uses it. A good idea can look terrific because of its packaging, the way it is presented to its prospective buyers. Or it can seem dull, drab, and miserable. Your "market" for ideas may be your immediate family and circle of friends. It might be your boss or co-workers. It might be someone you've never seen; someone you don't know.

One of this country's most successful life insurance salesmen once told me that his secret was that he sold himself, not the policies. What he meant was that he created trust and confidence in himself before he would talk about the advantages of his insurance.

Before you can build acceptance of your ideas, you've got to have people accept you, what you stand for, and what you say. This is accomplished by *sincerity*.

Here's how to work with sincerity and amaze people with your lightning-fast mental ability:

S—Smile when you greet your prospective customer.

I—Interest him by offering to give him something he needs.

N—Never insist that he listen.

C—Cause him to listen by making your presentation colorful.

E—Entice your listener with the benefits of your idea before you actually reveal the idea.

R—Reveal the idea with a flourish.

I—Ignore objections to the idea until you've finished explaining it.

T—Take the objections one at a time and show how they are not valid.

Y—You are the originator of the idea but you are giving it to your listener for his use.

Sincerity builds confidence in what you say and increases the validity of your presentation. Prepare your listener for acceptance of your idea with sincerity before you actually say what the idea is. Don't blurt out an idea before you've taken the S-I-N-C-E-R-I-T-Y steps. Prepare your customer or listener *in advance* by asking questions, submitting the facts, outlining the need for an idea such as the one you *will* suggest.

Just prior to your presentation of the idea, offer a little meditation or thought-form, asking for the necessary boost of Cosmosis energy to psychically bring about acceptance of your idea.

How Louise Won
a Brand New Car for an Idea

Louise T. won a brand new car for an idea she presented to her employer, an automotive manufacturer.

She noticed a better way to perform a certain car assembly operation in the plant where she worked. Asking for a Cosmosis boost, she received the psychic message, and she wrote down the suggestion and submitted it to the suggestion plan committee for consideration. The idea she had saved her company so much money that she was awarded a brand new car for one of the best ideas ever presented.

Louise uses the same Cosmosis method when she makes suggestions to her husband, children, and in-laws. It works like a charm every time. She has a reputation as a good "idea girl." People actually come to her for advice on their personal problems and she is the center of attraction because of her creative thinking and her unusual way of looking at things. Admiration and gratitude are shown wherever Louise goes. She is considering running for a position on her local school board.

How Felix Made a Suggestion
That Won a Promotion

Felix G. worked for an electronics manufacturer. He was an accountant who was very conscious of office procedures, forms, the "way" things were handled and routed. He found himself using Cosmosis to suggest changes, slight modifications, and improvements in the way his department was handling its accounts receivable. His boss was accepting his ideas enthusiastically.

After a year of continuous suggestions, most of which were put into practice immediately, Felix was called to his boss' office to be told that he was being given a promotion and a transfer to another division. It was the beginning of a very successful management career for Felix.

He continued to use the Cosmosis method of presenting winning ideas and his rise within the company was fast. Now he is an assistant vice-president, making well over $35,000 per year.

How Blanche Presented Winning Ideas to Her Husband

Blanche was the type that people laughed at. Her husband didn't pay much attention to her suggestions because he just couldn't see the merits of her thinking.

Blanche wanted to influence her husband's actions, particularly with respect to his spending habits. He tended to go "in over his head" for luxury items that consumed so much of the family budget that it was difficult for Blanche to pay the basic bills for rent, heat, light, and food.

She started making small suggestions at first. She presented a plan for meeting the basic bills by using the Cosmosis method. Then she gave him the idea of saving money for future purchases. Both of these ideas were accepted wholeheartedly by her husband. Others followed, and each idea met with greater and greater approval.

The marriage itself has improved tremendously since Blanche started presenting ideas that have amazed and pleased her husband.

HOW TO USE COSMOSIS FOR NEW VITALITY AND INSPIRATION

The talent and ability you have within you at this moment can be brought to light for others to see and appreciate if your personal power or vitality is constant. You need vitality and new inspiration to continue on, to build higher, to confidently step from one period of good luck to another. Cosmosis can give you the success when you use *affirmations for renewed vitality and inspiration.*

The fifth Cosmosis rule to follow to bring out the talent you already have is: *Use affirmations for inner strength, inspiration, and confidence-building.*

Here are some powerful affirmations that have worked wonders for others. They can help free you from "back-biting, jealous people," from "double-dealing," from every "negative concern" that is holding down your creativity or suppressing your true talent and ability.

Affirmation for Inner Strength—"O Infinite Spirit of Creativity and Talent, give me the Cosmosis energy to uphold my inner strength. I am strong now. I am free of care, worry, and negation. I am strong in my convictions, in my abilities, and in my thinking. Nothing can hold me back or prevent me from progressing with greater creativity, greater productivity, and greater talent. Cosmosis is in me now, touching every cell and fiber of my body with health. Cosmosis is in me now, renewing and regenerating every thought, action, decision, and realization."

Affirmation for Inspiration—"O Infinite Spirit of Invention and Originality, inspire me with new thoughts, new actions, and new realizations of my potential. I realize that I am a divine creature empowered to express my destiny in a multitude of ways. May the demonstrations of this divinity be renewed by Cosmosis, the energy of the universe, and may I be given the boldness to receive that which is waiting for me. I am inspired with good thoughts; I am inspired by right actions; I am inspired by the vastness of all creation."

Affirmation for Confidence-Building—"O Infinite Spirit of Confidence, create within me the will to be true to myself, the reason to know my potential, and the power to express confidence at all times. I am confident of my talent; I am confident of my ability; I am confident of all that I say, do, and think. Nothing can stop me in my progress to the top. Nothing can stop me from manifesting my divinity.

203

Nothing can stop me from demonstrating the great force of Cosmosis."

You have now added to your Cosmosis methodology the Cosmic keys to bringing out talent.

Nothing can prevent your ultimate conquest of life, as you are continually blessed and uplifted by Cosmosis. You have the techniques, the theory, the concrete ways of making your life what you want it to be.

You have at your command the greatest power that there is—Cosmosis!

You can call on this great power to meet any need and to create the manifested desires in you at this moment.

Points to Remember from This Chapter

To bring out talent, you need to follow these Cosmosis rules:

1. Don't be limited to thinking imposed by family, friends, and others you know.

2. Clear all levels of your mind and let your imagination explore all possible avenues of accomplishment.

3. Look for novel, unusual, or unique ways to do what you are doing now.

4. Before presenting a new idea, prepare your listeners for it through the Cosmosis approach.

5. Use affirmations in this chapter for strength, inspiration, and confidence-building.

Chapter 13

HOW TO STAY TUNED TO COSMOSIS

What should you do when you've finished this book? How can you demonstrate greater harmony within your being and in your life right away? What can you expect? Which Cosmosis program should you follow first?

Cosmosis gives you a more accurate understanding of your higher-mind powers and effective control of your life and destiny.

Staying tuned to Cosmosis means putting yourself in the driver's seat and then making sure that you *stay* there. Cosmosis is showing you the infinite possibilities of your life, the random, new, creative twists and turns which you have open to you. Gone will be the rigid, conventional, uncompromising self. *The transformed you is in the making. The power of the universe is at your command!*

THE CARDINAL RULES
OF PSYCHIC POWER

Two cardinal rules for staying tuned to Cosmosis are: (1) keep working at it, and (2) work at it in concert with other people. In other words, expect that there may be times when you *seem* to be standing still. Psychic powers are working underneath the surface during these so-called quiet periods. You may be advancing and not actually realize it. Keep on going. Keep your meditation up, continue to read, to grow, and be determined!

POOLING YOUR COSMOSIS ENERGY WITH OTHERS

The greatest advantage to working with other people is that a small group can pool its psychic resources. A psychic economy works in study groups. One person may be a little down one week and the others are able to supply the needed lift and inspiration. Later, another group member may feel "out of kilter" and may get just the gentle recharge of spiritual power necessary to carry on without depression or fatigue.

How Mrs. G.A. Got Out of a Psychic Slump

Mrs. G.A. was in a psychic slump. Prior to the slump she had been getting impressions in color, she had been healing herself and others, and her clairvoyant insight was of an excellent precognitive nature. Her development had started in a study group. And all of these wonderful psychic gifts had come to her within a short period of time. Mrs. G.A. allowed herself to be absent from the group for several weeks. Gradually, she began to notice that her psychic impressions were no longer in color. They came to her in black and white. She interpreted this as a clue that some of her energy was either being drained off or she was not up to par. She was also picking up quite a bit of negation. She found herself tuned in on negative thoughts about the future of the world, about herself, and about people she knew. She was in a rut, and she knew it.

206

She called to ask about it and I advised her to return to her group for several sessions.

She returned to her group and she was revitalized during the very first session. Here is what she described. "It was during our silent meditation. I felt as though an unearthly presence were in the room. It hovered over me. It looked like electricity. I could actually see it. Slowly the presence entered my body. It penetrated slowly into every part of my being. Suddenly I felt as though I were alone in space, just floating. Nothing could disturb or penetrate my calm state of just existing in space—unsupported, uncaring."

As the silent meditation came to a close, Mrs. G.A. not only felt uplifted, but also as though she had spent an entire night in a deep, restful sleep. Completely rejuvenated, she went home after the meeting and began to regain her former strength in psychic matters. She not only received impressions in vivid colors but demonstrated postcognitive understanding as well. Her ability to heal returned. She continued regular contact with her study group.

The experience of Mrs. G.A. is not unusual. When we are delighted and amazed with our new-found psychic abilities, we frequently think we can go it alone. But this is really an impossibility. In spite of all the quiet time, the personal meditations, and need for seclusion occasionally, it is almost imperative to keep in touch with others who are searching and seeking.

PROGRESSIVE UNFOLDMENT
WITH PSYCHIC POWERS

High watermarks in your unfoldment encourage further exploration and experimentation. Progression flows along on a plateau. Then it suddenly jumps onto a new wavelength or "changes gears." You may develop extrasensory perception and then find that mediumship comes along and you are able to communicate with discarnates. Or you may start out with an interest in mediumship and become an excellent healer. You may look for harmony in your life and locate financial prosperity instead. You may look for simple peace but you become aware of your capacity to channel love and encouragement to other people. Your original goal in Cosmosis study may change many times, and as it changes you will grow spiritually, mentally, and emotionally.

How Claude's Goal Changed to Clairvoyance

Claude was a small businessman who had franchised several ice cream parlors from a large company. He had selected locations with heavy traffic. Preliminary studies indicated that the places he had selected for his businesses potentially could be extremely profitable. He opened each of three stores simultaneously. He staged grand openings, gave away ice cream, had a drawing for a year's supply of dairy products, and presented all the people who attended with helium-filled balloons.

After several months of operation, he was worn to a frazzle. Business was not as good as he had expected. He found trouble hiring and managing employees. Inventory losses in one store were high. He had to run from one location to another in order to supervise and keep things together.

Claude entered a Cosmosis study group to help calm his nerves and learn how to demonstrate prosperity in his new business undertaking. But he learned something else instead.

About the eighth session, Claude got the impression that he had been in the group before. It was as though what was taking place had already happened to him and he was experiencing it again for the second time. When someone

208

said something, he would say, "I knew you were going to say that." This "déjà vu" feeling continued. It had a carry-over effect during his regular day. He would go to one of his stores and discuss a problem. It was as though he were an actor who had learned his lines so well that he could play this part by rote. This feeling continued for several weeks. Then it happened. Claude began to sense things before they took place. He knew that he would be doing a certain thing several days before he did it. In his search to calm his nerves and demonstrate prosperity, he had picked up clairvoyant ability to lift the veil and see slightly into the future. The ability didn't go much more ahead in time than several days. Claude explained, "It is like a hunch. I just know where I'm going to be needed or what needs to be checked up on." He permitted himself the luxury of being led by these clairvoyant flashes. He was at the right place at the right time. When he was needed at one of his stores, he was there. Intuitively, he made the right decisions. Claude's inner sensitivity made a business success out of him. Within a year's time, he was realizing a handsome profit on his investment in the ice cream parlors.

How April's Goal Changed to Healing

April, a high school student, started her study of extrasensory perception in order to foretell future events. The idea appealed to her as a good way to pass the time. Foretelling the future was good entertainment. Besides, her interest in psychic matters increased her personal popularity. Her friends at school became avidly interested in what she was doing, and the day after a group meeting she always described what had taken place to her circle of friends in the school's cafeteria.

April's friends asked her if she would be willing to start a little development group of her own. Seven of them got together once a week. Each one of the group became clairvoyant. They were quite pleased with their efforts as a group. A local minister asked them if they would also do intercessory prayer work for people who were in need of healing. In addition to their work with clairvoyance, they added a prayer period in which they sent out their healing thoughts and intentions for the names and conditions which were submitted to them. Some wonderful healing was set in motion by this little group of faithful teen-agers.

What had started out as one person's interest in foretelling the future turned out to be a dedicated commitment to help other people as well. Who knows what the far-reaching effects of this group will be if traced out over the next ten or 20 years? Each member may be a leader of another group and their simple techniques and discoveries may be transformed in some form to many people elsewhere. A small ripple can sometimes end up being a large wave.

How Bennett's Psychic Chain
Reaction Saved Him

A psychic chain reaction took place in the life of Bennett who started along the path of Cosmosis with *one* destination in mind. Before very long, he found himself at another destination—one that he would not have expected even in his wildest dreams. Bennett was a man with a single-purpose ambition. In his late forties when he happened onto psychic study, he had achieved a moderate success in life. He lived in a respectable suburb. He had a happy marriage and had raised three fine children. He was a middle-management executive with a large corporation. As he explained it, "I thought I had it made about the time I joined our local country club. My wife was active in charity work. The kids were married and settled. All I had left to do was ride out the tide. There wasn't anything that I wanted that I didn't have or couldn't get if I desired it."

But Bennett's state of equilibrium was rudely upset when he reached the conclusion that he had a problem with alcohol. He was powerless over it. It began to rule his life. He came apart at the seams slowly. It was probably more noticeable at work than at home, since alcohol was a natural part of his social life. But, he found himself taking long lunch hours and drinking enough to keep himself off-balance during the afternoon.

Bennett had heard about a psychic practitioner in town and made an appointment to "see what he could get." Of course his problem with alcohol was apparent and the practitioner told him so. He didn't really want to hear what was being said about the ultimate consequences of his habit and terminated the consultation without waiting for further impressions. He thought about the consultation. Maybe he did have a problem.

He decided to see me to find out if I would confirm what had been told to him in the previous interview.

It was all too clear to me that Bennett had a problem with alcohol and that it was about to take over his life. I explained to him that the problem was the single most important factor in his existence, since it could ruin everything that had taken years to build up.

"Why don't you get in touch with A. A.?" I asked finally.

"I'm not sure that my problem is that bad," he answered.

"Let's call A. A. and ask that someone stop by and see you anyway," I said.

Bennett agreed. I think we caught him at a moment when his guard was down, because the men from A. A. who visited him told him that the most difficult thing is to get someone to agree to see them. It implies an admission that there is a problem and most people don't want to admit that a problem exists. Bennett started on the A. A. program and has been dry for quite some time. His case simply shows

211

that a psychic chain reaction has many unexpected twists and turns.

A YEARLY UNFOLDMENT PLAN

As soon as you've finished this book, sit down and develop your Cosmosis plan,of study for the year.

Your yearly unfoldment plan can help you organize your development. Although you'll want to leave room for last-minute changes or unexpected developments, it can give you a guide by which you program yourself.

First make a list of the areas of Cosmosis study and practice that you'll want to work on.

You may decide to rearrange your yearly plan after you've started. Writing your program out, however, gives you a way to measure your advancement. With such a program, you know when you've reached a certain point and you have some idea what your next step or steps will be. You may want to use the chapters of this book as a basic guide, employing the techniques in each chapter, and then moving on to the next chapter.

The main thing is to *set your plan* and then *work it*.

A COSMOSIS CHECKLIST
FOR PSYCHIC DEVELOPMENT

Here are some questions to ask yourself as you follow your unfoldment plan. These questions will help you ascertain the *direction* in which you are moving.

1. During meditation do you have the feeling that there is something special that you are about to be shown that you should do?
2. Are you aware of spirit entities that may be attracted to you?

3. Do you sometimes have a desire to help someone who needs healing?

4. Do you get the feeling that you are about to really take hold of a plan to develop your psychic abilities?

5. Are you awakened during your sleep with a single thought uppermost in your mind?

6. Do you sense that someone is about to enter your life and have a profound effect on you and what you are doing at the present time?

7. Can you accept the positive, creative aspects of your inner psychic being?

8. Can you feel yourself as an instrument of the Cosmos waiting for direction from a source beyond yourself?

9. Is Cosmosis beginning to have a more constructive meaning for you?

10. Can you relax and let your extrasensory impressions guide you?

11. Do you realize your unique characteristics?

12. Can you feel yourself become a force for good?

The questions which you can answer in a positive way will indicate the direction of your life-force and the stage of your development. Let's break these questions down and see what they might suggest to you about your own progress.

Question # 1—An affirmative answer to this question indicates that your psychic sensitivity is opening up and that you are preparing yourself to be a psychic instrument.

Question # 2—An affirmative answer to this question indicates that you may be developing mediumship.

Question # 3—An affirmative answer to this question indicates that you may be developing healing gifts.

Question # 4—This question may indicate that you

are creating psychic harmony within your own self, which will lead to harmony in your exterior life.

Question # 5—This question answered affirmatively indicates that you are resolving conflicts and working out your repressed desires.

Question # 6—If you answered "yes" to this question, it points up your receptivity to psychic invention, your willingness to be led by events, rather than trying to manipulate them.

Question # 7—If you can accept yourself as a positive influence, you will begin to be a creative person who infuses all situations with love and acceptance.

Question # 8—"Yes" to this question indicates that you are already well along the pathway.

Question # 9—If you answer affirmatively to this question, you are advancing well.

Question # 10—This question answered affirmatively indicates that you have taken the first steps. If you answer this question in a negative way, or with some reservations, you need to start at the beginning and work slowly and carefully.

Question # 11—Your true selfhood is taking over if you can see this uniqueness.

Question # 12—If you answer this question affirmatively, you are becoming tuned to the universal aspects of your Cosmic nature.

HOW YOUR UNIQUE VALUE SYSTEM
WILL HELP

Cosmosis leaves the road open for you, to creativity and invention. Because of this, it implies that your value system will not be a rigid set of "do's" and "don't's" but, instead, it will be an imaginative system in Cosmic science that has great ranges of tolerances for other people and their shortcomings.

Because of your psychic understanding of other people, you will be demonstrating a flexible, adaptable way of looking at things since you will be able to see circumstances from the other person's point of view. Moreover, you won't be trying to force your value system on other people because you will realize that they, too, must find their own truth.

This way of looking at things will free you from preconceived attitudes and allow you to remain open until all of the evidence is in. You won't jump to conclusions or make snap judgements about yourself or other people. In short, you will be less critical. You will be more receptive, aware, and open, to experience all that life has to offer. Your life will be a series of exciting, wonderful events, each one more interesting and positive than the last. People will be attracted to you, and can well open doors for you, leading to health, wealth, and happiness in an overflowing quantity.

CHANGING YOUR WAVELENGTHS
TO GET MORE POWER

When you feel yourself getting a little stale, or depressed, or "dry," it is time to change wavelengths—to change your technique or try something more constructive. It may be that you've allowed your psychic powers to become a little self-centered. At times like this, seek out other people and new opportunities to make your advancement take on the thrill and excitement that it once had.

This is easy to do. A new book, a conversation with someone about some aspect of psychic power that appeals to you, or even a trip to another city will help. Meeting people from other locations does wonders to renew your psychic energy and your interest in proceeding along with your psychic powers.

You might want to vary your meditation or simply let

215

your psychic gifts rest for the time being while you recharge yourself with some other interests of a cultural nature.

Music, art, and literature, are all fine ways to renew and regenerate if you feel psychically bogged down. Many of our study group members make a point of planning social occasions outside their usual group meetings, in order to congregate and get to know and appreciate each other more.

USE A REFRESHER COURSE
TO GET STARTED AGAIN

One sure way to get yourself going after a lull period is to return to the basics. Try a simple meditation:

Repel negation.
Dwell on the positive.
Put your mind in a neutral, receptive state.

This three-step meditation can clear the way faster than any other.

Maybe you've neglected your dream writing pad temporarily and gotten yourself out of the habit of looking through your dreams into the deeper workings of your subconscious mind. Check into your subconscious thoughts.

Try putting your Cosmosis to work helping other people directly.

Give some kindly advice to someone in need.

Encourage a friend or relative in his hour of defeat or frustration.

Be as outgoing as you can. Keep your psychic energy level up, and don't try to work beyond your capacity to perform well.

When you feel a "dry" period coming on, just relax and seek out others.

It is inevitable that you will progress once you start your "upswing" again.

How Bill Renewed His Psychic Powers

Bill R. was developing accurate psychic insight. He hit a slump. Nothing psychic in nature came to him at all. He thought that his gift had left him entirely. He couldn't trace it to a single cause. He had been conducting his exercises without hesitation on a regular basis.

"I don't know what is causing it," he said to me.

"Is there anything that gave you a hint that this blockage could take place?" I asked.

"Nothing whatsoever," he answered.

"Maybe you are forcing yourself, pushing yourself too hard, expecting too much," I suggested.

"That might be. I've been going at it like an athlete training for a big event," he answered.

"Well, let's cut down on your psychic activity a little while," I answered. Bill began cutting his meditation time in half and by not paying such strict attention to his other psychic activities, he let himself be carried by the course of events and thought of himself as an observer rather than as an active, all-out participant.

This cutting back on Bill's participation seemed to do it. Within a few days, his former reliable guidance and direction was working. In fact, his intuitive powers were greater and more accurate than they had been before.

He said that he felt as though he was being carried along by his higher-mind powers, that they were directing him more and more. He was using the logical, reasoning faculties of his conscious mind to better advantage, too, because he was including data from his superconscious mind.

217

CONCLUSION

With the Cosmosis study you've just completed, you will find the rich experiences and personal rewards which all men seek. You are traveling the same pathways that sages and philosophers have followed from the beginning of time. The wisdom of mind and spirit is building the beauty, truth, and love which will eternally equip you for every situation. The pinnacles of achievement are waiting to be climbed. The challenges of discovery are waiting to be accepted. Every secret aspiration and hope is capable of being fulfilled.

Let these Cosmosis methods and techniques be a constant guide. Let them help you attract the profitable circumstances and sparkling friends which it is your right to have. Let them activate your mind and body with radiant health. Let them stimulate the opportunities and adventures that will create the blessings which spell happiness, contentment, peace of mind, and a vital life.

The secret of Universal Power has been unlocked for you.

219

Keep this magnificent force of Cosmosis working for you.

Master your life by using the natural laws of the universe which you've read about here. Overcome the apathy and lack of fulfillment which negates the entire lifetimes of millions of people. Break the bonds of a materialistic and selfish life and walk in the glorious destiny with the mighty ones.

If you elect the Cosmosis way of life, your every step will be guided, guarded, and protected. You cannot make a serious mistake or take a wrong turn. Everything you set out to do will be another demonstration of your charmed and lucky life.

The ending of this book means the beginning of your search for greater Cosmic understanding. So, in a sense, this book is not concluding, it marks the beginning for you.

You'll feel like a modern day pilgrim because you will be exploring inner space. Like the astro-scientist who charts the laws of outer space, you will become a mental scientist searching the domain of your inner mind. Your journey will be just as awe-inspiring as the journey of the men who rode a space vehicle to the moon.

I wish you luck, good health, prosperity, love, and fulfillment as you undertake your journey.